Sir Ian Botham is universally regarded [as one of the greatest] sporting characters, a man who trans[cends the game and] who lives life to the full. As England's [greatest all-rounder,] he amassed 102 caps and took a record 383 Test wickets. Since retiring from the game, he has become a much-loved commentator and an integral part of Sky Sports' cricket coverage, as well as raising millions of pounds for Leukaemia Research. His first autobiography was one of the biggest selling sports books of all time.

BEEFY'S CRICKET TALES

My Favourite Stories from On and Off the Field

Ian Botham

with Dean Wilson

SIMON &
SCHUSTER

London · New York · Sydney · Toronto · New Delhi

A CBS COMPANY

First published in Great Britain by Simon & Schuster UK Ltd, 2013
This paperback edition published by Simon & Schuster UK Ltd, 2014
A CBS company

5 7 9 10 8 6 4

Simon & Schuster UK Ltd
1st Floor
222 Gray's Inn Road
London WC1X 8HB

www.simonandschuster.co.uk

Simon & Schuster Australia,
Sydney

Simon & Schuster India,
New Delhi

A CIP catalogue record for this book is available from the British Library

ISBN: 978-1-84983-801-6
Ebook ISBN: 978-1-84983-802-3

Typeset in the UK by Hewer Text UK Ltd, Edinburgh
Printed in the UK by CPI Group (UK) Ltd, Croydon, CR0 4YY

Foreword

Remembering and committing to paper a collection of cricket stories for a book like this has been a long-held ambition of mine, because the game simply has so many tales to tell.

These are the stories that are told up and down the land in bars after matches and in after-dinner speeches, and are the memories that we as pros hold on to. And when your career is finally over, that is what you have left – the memories.

The statistics on a piece of paper and the medals in your trophy cabinet are great things to treasure, but they are there to remind you of what happened and what you achieved. This book is an attempt in some small way to record some of the memories that came out of being in a cricket dressing room and the fun you had. Often the moments that bring back the widest grin are not the fours or sixes that you've hit but the pranks and jokes that occur off the field, and you'll get to read all about them in this book.

My first and biggest thank-you has to go to all the players, past and present, who have agreed to share their stories first hand within these pages. There are plenty of anecdotes that can never be told, and each player knows only too well what must stay behind closed doors, but in each of these instances they have been as forthcoming as possible to give you a real feel for what goes on in a cricket dressing room.

I think some have quite enjoyed the chance to tell the odd story about me, too, even though I don't always come out looking the best. But that's okay, since you've got to be able to take it as well as give it, and I certainly gave it plenty during my playing days!

These guys are the ones who have made this collection of anecdotes possible and for that I am very grateful. I owe them all a huge debt of thanks for relaying their tales to my ghostwriter Dean Wilson, who has put them together in a sensible and coherent way.

Deano has worked with me for over seven years now and I couldn't have wished for a better ghost to help me put my words into print. He has been able to work seamlessly with the other players while squeezing what he could out of my fading memory banks.

His company throughout this process, along with a well-chosen bottle of wine, has made it a labour of love and I thank him heartily for that.

Of course I must thank my supportive family, especially my wife Kath, who will have seen and heard a fair few of these stories herself over the years but still indulges my retelling of them with a smile and maybe a roll of the eyes.

Thanks also to the team at Simon and Schuster, especially Ian Marshall and Rhea Halford, who helped bring this project to life and guided it through from idea to finished book. It has all been appreciated.

Now to go and have some more fun!

Contents

Contents

Contents

Contents

Introduction

With well over 40 years in the game behind me, I've been involved with, seen and heard of everything that can go on within the four walls of a dressing room. Sometimes it hasn't been pretty, but on the vast majority of occasions it has been interesting, funny, or both.

Dressing rooms can be unusual places for the uninitiated, largely because they resemble a group of men who have failed to grow up properly. The humour is childish, the banter is puerile, the jokes largely born out of a playground mentality where kids tend to hunt in packs.

Yet almost every person who has lived some of their life in a cricket dressing room has got one thing in common. They can do things on a cricket field that the rest of the Great British Public can only dream of, and that is why they are loved. They are capable of great feats of endurance and skill, incredible concentration, determination and power all under immense pressure. Perhaps that is why we like to unwind with fun and frolics, usually accompanied with a glass or two of our favourite tipple.

In this book you will read about some of those antics, and between me and my fellow pros we've tried to give you a flavour of just what it is like to be a professional cricketer.

There are tales from yesteryear from the likes of David Lloyd, Bob Willis and of course yours truly, but we come right up to the present with current England stars like Matt Prior and Steven Finn revealing what they get up to on and off the field these days too.

Before each story kindly retold within these pages I've offered one or two thoughts about the men retelling them. Some of them I've shared a dressing room with and others I've commentated on, but one thing binds them all together and that is their love of the game.

What shines through is that no matter how much the game changes – and, let's face it, the cricket being played in T20 matches now bears little resemblance to a Test match in the 1970s – the behaviour of cricketers has largely remained the same. The practical jokes that made us laugh 30 years ago still work a treat now, although perhaps the number of late nights has come down a notch or two.

What is also apparent is that no matter where you played your cricket, be it England, Australia or India, the dressing room retains its unwritten rules of behaviour. The characters that brought the dressing room to life an age away are still there causing mayhem and laughter, and the truth is the game needs these types of players to keep hold of the sport's rich tapestry. It is something I hope never changes.

I've had such a good time playing and being involved in the game that my only hope is that players starting out today can still get just as much fun and satisfaction from it as I did. This is a book to celebrate those moments of brilliance on the field and the fun that goes with it off the field, and when all is said and done, cricket remains the greatest game of them all. I hope you enjoy it.

Beefy

In no other sport is the captain as important as he is in cricket and in that regard England have been blessed to have had some of the greatest minds in charge of the national team over the years. Right up there in a list of the great skippers must surely come Michael Atherton, not because he won more matches than anyone else or was the best tactician the game had ever seen, but because during a period of incredible instability for the team, and a run of some dreadful results, he stood firm and refused to be cowed or broken, leading his team by high-quality example. The 1990s were as tough as it got for English cricket and especially if you were a batsman facing up to the likes of Ambrose and Walsh, Donald and Pollock or Wasim and Waqar. Athers stood up to them all, tried his hardest to bring success to his side and on occasion did just that. Since he's retired as a player, he's become one of the most respected and thought-provoking pundits on the game and a fine journalist to boot. Still, all those brains can't stop him making some ridiculous comments in the Sky commentary box and at least I'm there to put him right!

MICHAEL ATHERTON – STAND UP FOR YOURSELF

Looking back on my career as a professional and international cricketer, I have been in countless battles on the field and, if I'm honest, I thrived on it.

As an opening batsman you have to have a certain amount of courage and desire to take on the world's fastest bowlers and not only survive but succeed. I revelled in that challenge and even though you can't expect always to come out on the right side of those contests, when you did there was a great sense of satisfaction in your achievement.

It was the cut and thrust of that duel which made for the most interesting aspect of my job, and occasionally it would provide moments of intense drama for the spectators.

The battle which appears to have stood out most for the general public was the one between Allan Donald and myself during 1998 when we were both at the peak of our powers as cricketers. AD was a fearsome quick bowler, dubbed 'white lightning', and had more than enough pace to back up that nickname. I had enjoyed some success against the South Africans in the past so there was a rivalry bubbling away, and it all came to a head during the fourth Test at Trent Bridge during what was the most intense piece of cricket I have ever been involved in. With AD bowling round the wicket at me, bowling at the speed of light, he was getting more and more worked up because a) he managed to take my glove but the umpire didn't spot it and gave it not out, and then b) Nasser Hussain was dropped by Mark Boucher, at which point he let out an almost primeval scream.

It was cricket at its most raw and looking back on it now I'm glad I was a part of it. The wonderful thing about it was that at the end of the game, AD came into the dressing room and we had a beer together and were able to chat and laugh about it. The mutual respect was obvious – he knew I wasn't a batsman he could scare into submission, and I knew he wasn't a bowler to take liberties with. While we were talking about that passage of play I showed him exactly where he had managed to beat me because there was a clear red mark on my glove, and he laughed.

He laughed even harder when I asked him to sign the offending mark, and he did so without a problem.

I still see AD every now and again on the cricket circuit. He is working with the South African team as their bowling coach while I am working as a journalist, and that mutual respect and friendship born out of the white heat of Test cricket is a special thing to treasure. Facing AD was one of the biggest battles I had on the field but I learnt very early on that I would also have to deal with one or two issues off the field, and they can be found in all corners of the dressing room.

Right at the start of my career in the Lancashire team I was presented with a little scenario that told me a lot about how dressing rooms work. Back in the 1980s there were a few strong characters at Old Trafford and none more so than Paul 'Walt' Allott and Graeme 'Foxy' Fowler, internationals both. They pretty much ran the dressing room and quite a few of the younger players were a little fearful of them. They certainly gave guys like Ian Folley a bit of a torrid time. I didn't really know too much about it as a fresh-faced lad coming straight from Cambridge University.

Thankfully there were others who were a bit more helpful and Neil Harvey Fairbrother was one. He pulled me to one side and told me that if I showed weakness and let Walt and Foxy boss me around then they would make my life a misery and would be all over me from that point on. It was a message I took on board and I was determined not to be pushed around.

It was during my first Roses match at Headingley against Yorkshire that I got the chance to put my resolve into practice. In the old dressing rooms that used to be square of the wicket, there was a small clothes dryer for players to use and on this particular day I had a few bits and bobs in there, a jockstrap and some socks and a T-shirt. During the lunch break we had just come in from a session in the field – Walt had been bowling and he wanted to put some things of his own in the dryer. He opened it, took out my stuff, flung it across the dressing room and put his kit in there instead. Well, I wasn't having that. So I marched over to the dryer and removed his items and put mine back in. Walt looked at me and then at Foxy, but he didn't do anything. He just sat there.

After the day's play we all got changed and Walt said to me, 'All right, youth, Foxy and me are going to have a drink in Bradford on the way back – do you want to join us?' I thought I'd arrived. They'd clearly been impressed by my earlier actions, standing up to them the way I did, and this was their way of saying I was all right.

We went to the Novotel in Bradford and strolled up to the bar. As Walt and I ordered our drinks, Foxy said to get him a pint as he had to nip off to the loo. Just as the drinks arrived, Walt said he needed to go and relieve himself as well. So there I was, sat at the bar with three drinks, waiting for the other two to officially welcome me into the Lancashire team. Five minutes passed and no sign of them. It slowly dawned on me that far from treating me as one of them, they had left me stranded in Bradford. As a poor student, I had no money even to pay for the drinks let alone get a taxi back to Leeds.

In a panic I legged it out of the bar and into the hotel car park, searching frantically for my 'team-mates', at which point I noticed their car pulling on to the main road.

Never before or since have I run as fast as I did that day, and thankfully there was enough traffic to hold them up and I caught up with the car. I banged on the door and pleaded with them to let me in. They looked straight ahead. I kept banging, but they drove off down the road. Midway through cursing their very existence, the car pulled over about 20 metres up the road and, with all the relief of a child who has found its parents in the supermarket, I jumped in and they took me back.

From that point on I knew not to mess with them and they too knew that this university kid would not be pushed around. We've got on famously ever since.

Full credit to anyone who makes it to the pinnacle of their chosen sport and in that regard Rob Bailey did just that, playing four Test matches for England. His misfortune was that, with a tour to India cancelled in 1988, all four of those games were against the rampant West Indians of the 1980s and early 1990s. The game is littered with the remains of batsmen steamrollered by those quick men, but after a taste in 1988 he came back for more and, if luck had gone his way, perhaps he could have had a go against another opponent. As it was he turned his attentions instead to Northamptonshire, where he was a county hero for more than 15 years. He is now an accomplished umpire, experiencing international cricket again – and he will last much longer this time.

ROB BAILEY – YOU WIN SOME, YOU LOSE SOME

People have described me as an unlucky cricketer, because I played in just four Test matches, missed out on an India tour and was then on the end of a shocking decision when I got recalled. But actually I think I'm quite fortunate. I'm lucky to have played the game I love for the best part of 20 years professionally and am still involved in it now as an umpire. I can't be too upset with that.

Take me back to spring 1990 and I'd give you a different answer, but time is a great healer. I thought I had acquitted myself reasonably well against the Windies in 1988, scoring 43 at The Oval and doing enough to get myself on the winter tour to India. Then came the gut-wrenching news that I, along with several other players, wouldn't be granted a visa to tour India because of a connection with South Africa. I had played club cricket there and done a bit of coaching at the age of 18. I had no idea the situation with apartheid would affect me when it came to my professional career.

I so desperately wanted to play for England again after that first taste and when the tour was called off on political grounds I thought my chance had gone. The hopes of a replacement tour were dashed, and even though the TCCB – as the ECB was called at the time – paid us our tour fee to make that winter a little easier, I was still pining for England honours and I feared they would never come again.

As it happens I was offered the opportunity to join a rebel tour to South Africa the following year, but I turned it down because I still thought I could make it as an England player and I couldn't face being banned and throwing that possibility away.

Despite a difficult 1989 summer for Northamptonshire I was picked for that winter's tour to the Windies. I hoped I would restart the Test career so unfortunately paused. That chance came in the third Test in Trinidad. Things were looking good for us – we were one up in the series and we managed to draw this one. However, for me it wasn't exactly the grand return to the game I was hoping for – a pair of ducks is no fun at any time but to get them when you're so desperate to succeed is a body blow. Still, I kept my place for the next Test in Barbados and here I managed to do a little better – but only a little! Getting 17 runs in the first innings before being bowled by Ian Bishop was a small victory bearing in mind where I'd come from, but we needed more from our No. 3 and I knew it.

We were fighting for our lives, up against a West Indian team not used to anything but winning. The pressure on us was immense, but truth be told it was even more so on the Windies, who were getting a bit of a kicking from their own press for not putting us away. It was against this backdrop that I unintentionally got caught up in a bit of a scandal. We were set the highly unlikely target of 365 to win, but the real task was to try and bat out the remainder of the fourth and fifth days to secure a hard-fought draw.

Allan Lamb had batted brilliantly for a hundred in the first innings and everyone was looking to him and Robin Smith to be two of our heroes. I wanted to be another.

The first 15 minutes went without too much of a hitch. The crowd were baying for English blood and both Ian Bishop and Curtly Ambrose were steaming in, looking to satisfy that hunger.

Now, I knew Curtly well from having played at Northants with him for the previous two years. He was a terrific bowler and mean with it. I was so glad he was on my side most of the time. He wasn't exactly a gentle giant off the field either; he was his own man, he did things the Curtly way and you had to live with it. But he respected the game and his team-mates hugely and he gave it everything when he bowled.

With designs on saving this match, my contest with Curtly was one I had to win, and I was doing so until one moment that changed everything. He sent one fizzing into the body; I managed to miss the ball, but it brushed my hip and went through to Jeff Dujon. It was the last ball of the over and the umpire, a Mr Lloyd Barker, appeared to be walking off to square leg. Out of nowhere Viv Richards appealed like a screaming banshee and did a little dance to go with it. It was described in the *Wisden Cricketers' Almanack* report like this: '*Bailey was given out in controversial circumstances by umpire Barker after a charging finger-flapping appeal by Richards which was at best undignified and unsightly. At worst, it was calculated gamesmanship.*'

Now, I cannot and will not say that Mr Barker changed his mind on the back of that appeal, but I will say that I was very surprised to see the finger go up soon after.

There was an outcry in our dressing room after that episode, but the Windies crowd loved it and with all the pressure Viv was under, he helped get a wicket his team needed. I was so angry I went back to the pavilion and took my frustration out on the fridge with my right boot. I broke my toe.

It wasn't a bad break; I was still able to play in the next match, albeit moving rather gingerly at times. I wasn't about to give up on my Test career that easily. As it turned out, the fifth Test in Antigua was my last match for England. A return of 42 in the first innings wasn't bad, but we still ended up losing by an innings as Curtly ran through us in the second.

I was still seething from the way he had got me out in the previous match and since we were on opposite teams there was no conversation before we left for home. The following summer the Windies toured England but, as there was no match against Northamptonshire in their itinerary, it wasn't until the next year that I finally got the chance to talk to Curtly about the incident. I had calmed down somewhat by then, but even if I hadn't I don't think I could have stayed upset with him when he came straight up to me, put his huge arm around my shoulder and said, 'Rob, man. You win some, you lose some. That's cricket.' He followed it up with a big grin and we were back to normal again.

Tim Bresnan is the sort of player in the current era who I think would have fitted into my England dressing room without any problem at all. He is a burly bowling all-rounder who has cricket in his blood. You'd have to if you'd played the game professionally since the age of 16. He is now a mainstay of England's three teams and it feels like he's been around forever. He's a big no-nonsense Yorkshire lad who bowls a heavy ball and I think some batsmen are surprised at how fast he can bowl it because he almost ambles in before letting it go. He can bat, too, and to my mind there is nothing better than a bloke who has just taken five wickets and then walks out and smashes the bowling all round the park. That is Bressie for you.

TIM BRESNAN – THE YORKSHIRE SNIPPER

As a young player making my way through the junior teams at Yorkshire, all I ever wanted to do was make it into the first team at Headingley. Representing my county was what it was all about. I had grown up with stories about the great Yorkshire players of the past – Boycott, Illingworth, Close, Bairstow, Sidebottom to name a few – so when I realised I had a bit of ability and could bowl, it became my total focus. I didn't really think I would play for the first team as quickly as I did, but I had no doubts that it was the place for me.

Going from the junior dressing room and into the senior side can be a bit daunting, especially when you looked around at some of the faces, men like Darren Gough, Craig White, Matthew Hoggard and Anthony McGrath – England internationals one and all.

Thankfully the Yorkshire dressing room was a good one, full of great characters and banter, which I loved even as a kid.

One of the things you hear about when you're on the fringes of the first team is the 'Yorkshire snipper', and it has been going on for years. You're told that the snipper exists, that no one knows who he is, but every now and then he'll take a pair of scissors to someone's clothes and leave them with half of what they had before. Socks are the favourite item, but nothing cuttable is safe.

During my first couple of seasons I was lucky enough not to be 'snipped' too many times; I just kept my head down and got on with playing the game. Others were less fortunate.

Our overseas player came from Australia, a premier batsman called Darren Lehmann, who was not only a brilliant cricketer but a top bloke as well. Everyone calls him 'Boof' for his obvious ability to hit a cricket ball. He was serious on the field and he could also at times be a bit serious off it too, so when he fell foul of the snipper he was not impressed. But he took it with good grace since it was part and parcel of the Yorkshire spirit and the dressing room – he just wasn't quite sure *why* we did it.

The snipping would often happen when we had suffered a tough day in the field or needed a bit of a lift, and because of Darren's reaction he was a good target. After one snipping, he really lost it and demanded to know who the snipper was, but no one came forward. He accused Anthony McGrath because he was laughing so much, but there was no joy there. After a spot of detective work, Boof heard that our fast bowler Steve Kirby was a likely suspect, and his suspicions grew even more the next time he was snipped. He decided to take matters into his own hands and pay him back.

Steve used to drive a black luxury car and was pretty pleased with it. One morning, Boof was being driven into the ground and was hanging out of the passenger window looking for Steve. He spotted him on the balcony, and at that point pulled out a car aerial and started cleaning his teeth as though it were a toothpick.

'Recognise this, snipper?' said Boof, looking pleased as punch with his new flossing tool.

'What do you mean?' replied Steve.

'Don't you recognise your car aerial, snipper? I picked it up this morning outside the hotel. Without the radio, it will give you a chance to think about what you've done,' said Boof with a satisfied smile.

'Dunno what you're talking about, mate, my car's been in the ground car park overnight!'

Boof's face dropped as he realised what he'd done – stolen a random car aerial from somebody else's car. Naturally the dressing room enjoyed the fact that our Aussie player had just done the sort of thing that would have seen him transported to Australia, not all that long ago.

If the owner of that car is reading this, Boof is very sorry and he is currently the coach of Australia!

I'm told that people refer to the 1981 Ashes as 'Botham's Ashes' on account of a few decent performances from yours truly, and in much the same way the 2005 series is remembered for Freddie Flintoff's exploits. There is always someone who emerges as the hero over a five-match series and in 1986/87 that man was Chris Broad, who collected three hundreds as we shocked everyone bar ourselves by beating Australia in their own back yard. Broady was a good man to have in your team; totally focused on his job, he hated giving his wicket away cheaply and that is exactly what you want from your opening batsman. His secondary career as an ICC match referee was an interesting move for one who had his own fiery temper, but he has proven himself to be just as good in a suit as he was in his whites.

CHRIS BROAD – VERY SUPERSTITIOUS

Sportsmen can be a superstitious bunch, and cricketers especially so. Everyone has their own spot in the dressing room where they get changed and woe betide the new boy if he tries to muscle in on someone's turf. There are plenty of lucky socks, jockstraps and shirts that have given players comfort throughout their careers. It is of course utter nonsense, but if there is something that mentally helps players perform at their best then why stop them? Superstition can, however, spread through a team and lead to some awkward situations, like in the Benson and Hedges Cup final of 1989.

Despite being a long-serving member of the Nottinghamshire team and playing my part in getting us to the final that year, I was not allowed to watch it live with my team-mates on the balcony. And for those of you who remember the dramatic finale, it was precisely because of the close nature of the game that I was denied the chance to watch it properly.

It was during a period when we seemed to meet Essex in the final of cup competitions quite a bit and both teams enjoyed their successes. Four years earlier we had played them in another close NatWest final, which they had won by just one run, so both teams badly wanted to win this one.

Essex had set us 244 to chase in 55 overs, which was a decent score in those days, and it all came down to the final over and then the final ball. That over must have taken at least 12 minutes to bowl because they kept changing the field settings. John Lever, aka 'JK', was the bowler and Eddie Hemmings the batsman. Eddie only really had one shot, which was square of the wicket on the off side. As a result they brought up Brian Hardie from the off-side boundary into the ring and JK bowled almost the perfect leg stump yorker. Yet somehow Eddie managed to get it to the boundary and win the game.

I'm telling you all this as a bloke who was there, but I only know what happened because team-mates were shouting to me through the dressing-room door. During the final 10 overs no one was allowed to move lest it disrupt the overall karma.

I was lying on the couch in the away team dressing room and as the game got closer and closer I wanted to go out on to the balcony with my team-mates and watch the play unfold. But the superstitious members of the team held sway and told us all to stay put because any movement would be bad for the team, as if that had anything to do with it! I should have told them to get stuffed, but the fact I stayed where I was showed that even more rational sportsmen can believe in lady luck and a bit of superstitious help. You'll do anything to help your team win and if that means missing out on watching the finale, then so be it. The fact that we won the game off the last ball of the match proved the point – or so I'm told.

It was a great moment for our team and our dressing room, which had been through a bit of upheaval the year before. We had lost quite a few players in 1988 – and some special players at that. Guys like Clive Rice and Richard Hadlee had gone after years of amazing service, and it was left to Tim Robinson to skipper us through the period. Unfortunately for him, things didn't really go his or the team's way and we were really struggling. We were getting beaten for fun by teams we knew weren't as good as us, but we just weren't performing.

One morning on the final day of a game against Worcestershire in July, we were having our warm-up jog around the outfield when Tim turned to me and told me how difficult he was finding it. We were chatting about the rut we'd got into and he didn't really know how we would get out of it. He wasn't sure what to do next and I said to him, 'Why not resign?' He clearly wasn't enjoying the job and the team wasn't responding to him. He didn't really react or say anything, so I thought nothing more of it.

Ahead of us was a tough task. We needed 224 to win when Worcestershire had been 39 for eight in their first innings and we had been 47 for eight in ours. To say the odds were stacked against us was an understatement. Tim and I opened up and a few overs later I was back in the hutch for just four, but Tim went on to score a tremendous not out hundred to win the game. It was just what we needed.

After taking all the congratulations from everyone when he came back into the dressing room he called a team meeting. Not just the team, but he called the whole squad in.

He didn't mention me by name but he said: 'It has been suggested to me that with the way things have been going that I resign. I want to know what sort of support I have in the dressing room?'

No more than four or five hands went up to support him so he resigned on the spot. This understandably caused a bit of a stir, but for the most part the dressing room thought it a reasonable move and said so with their show of hands. The committee were having none of it, though. Tim was their man and they would decide when he stopped doing the job, not the players.

My team-mate John Birch and I used to go to the pub next door for a drink after a game and, this being a good win, we did our usual thing and went and sank a couple. We were spied by some committee members who assumed that we must have been colluding against Tim, and for the great crime of having a beer after a game I became perceived as a troublemaker and they made it clear they wanted Robinson to continue as captain. Part of his agreeing to come back as captain, though, was that he didn't want me in the first team, so I was dropped to the second team for two weeks as a slap on the wrists for suggesting he resign, even though the rest of the team had concluded the same thing.

I was pretty angry about it at the time, but looking back I suspect it galvanised Tim to improve as a captain and he actually became a better one. The success we had the following year at Lord's was just rewards for him and a great moment for the club, even if I wasn't allowed to watch!

DON'T MESS WITH VIV

Having lived with and played with and against Viv Richards all my cricketing life, I knew just how good he was. I also knew just how ferocious his temper could be and why it was a good idea to stay on the right side of him whenever possible. He tormented and punished so many bowlers as a batsman in his pomp that many were just glad of the chance to bowl at someone else.

Viv also had a good idea about how the game should be played and when people crossed a line it would get him very annoyed. He would be the first to admit that there were times when he might have pushed the boundaries himself, but if he did, then he would take whatever flak came his way and move on. He never lost that burning desire to do well and to show people how good he could be, and it stayed with him until the very last.

His final season as a professional cricketer was in 1993 for Glamorgan and it was a year to remember, as he helped them win their first piece of silverware for 24 long years. A fiercely proud club for a fiercely proud man – and it came together in that season with the Sunday League trophy wending its way to Sophia Gardens.

The way the season panned out meant that the final game of the Sunday League was a winner-takes-all shoot-out between Kent and Glamorgan down in Canterbury. As was the case in those days the Sunday League match would be sandwiched in between the championship match, usually between days three and four. After a washout on the Thursday, play started on the Friday with Kent batting. They had the great Carl Hooper in their team and they piled on the runs, with Hoops scoring a brilliant double hundred. On the Saturday they declared on 524 for six and were in total command of the game. When Glamorgan came in to bat they were skittled – all out for 144 in 46 overs. It was a job well done.

What should have happened next was for Kent to enforce the follow-on and try to win by an innings. Instead, with half an eye on the Sunday League match the next day they chose to bat again, the theory being that they would save the energy in their bowlers' legs and keep them fresh for the other game. That did not go down well in Viv's eyes, who thought it was wrong for them to be playing the match thinking about another competition. If they wanted to rest their bowlers then they didn't have to play them in the championship tie at all, but having done so Viv thought they should play the game properly.

He was clearly upset about the tactic and that evening, after play had finished, he let his temper get the better of him. Standing on the Glamorgan balcony that looked straight into the Kent dressing room, he shouted at them: 'If you f**k with the game, the game will f**k with you!!'

The Kent boys thought they were witnessing the ramblings of a past-it player who couldn't do the things he used to. They laughed in his face. Well, I could tell them for free that it probably wasn't the best idea they'd ever had.

The next day, 13,000 people swarmed into the St Lawrence ground to watch their fresh Kent heroes send the great

Viv Richards off into retirement empty-handed. Some of the Glamorgan players had to park their cars on the road and walk the final few hundred metres to the ground, it was so busy.

Kent even managed to bat first and give their bowlers a bit more time with their feet up, but a score of 200 for nine in their 50 overs wasn't exactly earth-shattering. Glamorgan responded with a well-paced run chase thanks to a fifty from Hugh Morris, but when he was the third man out for 67 with the score at 98 for three there was still plenty to be done. Enter Viv to a generous standing ovation as he settled in for one of his last professional knocks.

With the ball in his hand stood Duncan Spencer, a tearaway fast bowler who had just dismissed Matthew Maynard and had pinned Adrian Dale in the ribs with a ball that was to leave a bruise for about a year. Viv still refused to wear a helmet and in his dark blue Glamorgan cap fronted up to the quick man. It was fast and hostile, and Spencer even managed to sneak one through Viv's gloves and rap him in the chest, too.

A few of the Kent boys took the chance to remind him of his outburst the night before and he just smiled, marked his guard and set to work. It was a terrific atmosphere and the last high-profile match that Viv was to play. By the time he left the field he had a match-winning 46 not out to his name, a stump in his hand and a Sunday League trophy to collect.

Kent learnt their lesson that day. If you mess with Viv Richards, then Viv Richards will mess with you.

It is called the England and Wales Cricket Board, but that doesn't mean we don't like seeing the odd Irishman or Scot pulling on the shirt, especially when they're as committed and as wholehearted as Dougie Brown was. A useful fast-medium bowling all-rounder, he was part of one of the most successful county sides of all time in the Warwickshire dressing room of the 1990s. Strong performances got him into the England one-day team and while he never quite made it to the Test arena, he rightly deserved his honours. Now he has transferred that hard-working attitude to being a coach and, as the director of cricket back at Warwickshire, he can put into practice what he learnt at the club under men like Bob Woolmer and John Inverarity, adding his own twist on things. I can only think that the Bears will be better for having him in charge. In addition, there is a great story about him on page 272 which I think reveals the character of the man. Someone you'd want to have with you on a night out!

DOUGIE BROWN – PAUSING FOR DIM THOUGHT

When you're in a cricket team there is always a distinct pecking order. At the top you have the legends of the game, the men like Brian Lara, Allan Donald or Sachin Tendulkar, the real 'greasts'. Then you have the senior pros, perhaps current internationals or former internationals; they are followed by the county stalwarts and solid performers; and finally come the emerging talents and the youngsters trying to break into the team.

That is just how it works and it is much the same in any walk of life. It doesn't mean that you are more or less a part of the team; it is just a reflection of what you've achieved. When I played for Warwickshire in the mid-1990s there was one man I looked up to more than any other and that was Allan Donald or 'AD'. This guy was a supreme athlete, an unbelievable bowler and probably the most competitive man I've ever met. People have told me that I'm hugely competitive and always give everything. Well, that is because I learnt it from the master. It didn't matter if it was a wet Wednesday in the championship in May or a sunny Saturday in a Lord's Test match in August, AD always gave it his all. You might think that it just isn't possible, but somehow AD got himself up for bowling no matter where he was or who he was against, and there are plenty of batsmen with plenty of bruises to prove it.

As a fast bowler myself it was one of the greatest honours of my career to open the bowling with him for Warwickshire for a couple of seasons. I learnt so much from him and the way he went about his business. He was the ultimate professional and, although he was classed as an 'overseas' player for the club since he was tearing in for South Africa, he was anything but. He was and is as much a part of the Warwickshire furniture as Dennis Amiss or Ashley Giles.

He was also a lovely guy off the field, too. Always keen to help and to pass on his knowledge, which is why it comes as no surprise that he is now a successful international bowling coach with his former team. But those who remember his fearsome spells on the field will understand that he was quite a different animal if he was bowling against you. He was mean, moody and hugely aggressive – you didn't want to mess with AD once he got into his zone and was after a batsman.

One day we were playing up at Northampton and AD was in the middle of a lengthy spell and had bowled us to the brink of victory. We needed one last wicket to win and he was charging in, giving it everything.

For those unfamiliar with Wantage Road, back in those days it was a huge expanse of grass which the cricket club shared with the football club and it was effectively open on one side. They would separate the grounds using advertising hoardings, so off to one side the football would be played and beyond that were the stands for people to watch the game. Obviously, being so far away, they were not used for cricket matches. That didn't stop our wicket-keeper, Keith Piper, posing the question to the slip cordon: 'Lads, how do the people sat in that stand over there know what is going on if they are so far away? How do they get to watch the game?'

Quick as a flash Dermot Reeve, standing at slip, said: 'Well, Pipes, it is because in each seat there is a set of opera glasses for them to look through.'

'Oh, right, I see. I haven't been to the opera for ages, but I do love it. My gran used to take me.'

At which point there was a double take from the entire cordon – Nick Knight at second slip, Dominic Ostler at third and me in the gully. I should explain that none of us were opera types, and certainly not Pipes. This was a lad who grew up in north London and was a bit of a tearaway and found cricket as the perfect outlet. He was not a man for the opera.

'So, Pipes, what is your favourite opera then? *Madame Butterfly*? *La Bohème*?' Dermot asked.

'It will come to me,' said Piper.

Meanwhile AD was sending down these thunderbolts and was in a great rhythm. As he came in to bowl for maximum effort, he got as far as the umpire when Pipes held up his glove and shouted, 'Whoa! Whoa! Wait!'

AD pulled out of his delivery stride with a murderous face, having just sprinted 25 metres for nothing. He looked at Pipes as if to say, 'This'd better be good.'

'I've got it,' declared Pipes. 'It was *Dick Whittington*!'

AD would have throttled him there and then if it wasn't for the fact that the entire slip cordon were in stitches, rolling around with laughter at their 'cultured' wicket-keeper. Pipes was very proud of himself and couldn't understand why everyone was in hysterics. And to this day no one has corrected him.

Guys like AD and Dermot were the senior men in that dressing room and they would help the younger guys along and teach them the things that you take for granted when you've been around for a few years. It is perhaps easy to forget how young and naïve you were when you started out and, in my role as a coach now, I try to make sure that the next generation are not only taught how to play the game technically but also how to be smart on and off the cricket field. Despite this, one or two bits of information slip through the net.

A couple of years ago a young bowler by the name of Maurice Holmes was making his debut for the club against Scotland at Edgbaston. It was a roasting hot day and we were in the field first. He was extremely nervous and when you're nervous you tend to do what you can to take your mind off things, whether it is having a drink or whatever. He signalled for the 12th man to bring on a towel about 10 overs into the innings. It seemed a bit strange, especially as he hadn't even bowled yet. The 12th man ran on with the towel, handed it to him and watched as he wiped it on his trousers and inside his trouser leg and then threw it back at him.

Puzzled by this and wondering whether he had spilled something on himself, we were taken aback by what had actually happened. It turned out that Maurice was so nervous he needed the toilet, but because it was his debut he was too scared to ask to go off the field. So, he pretended to do a bit of stretching and as he was laid out, he relieved himself on the outfield and thus required the towel.

We now make sure that every player, young and old, knows that if they need the toilet after the first or the 100th over, then off they come. There are some things you just assume players would know . . .

Every top international batsman is defined by at least one incredible innings. It is their signature knock which shows everyone just how good a player they are. The better the player, the more of this kind of innings you have – goodness knows how many Brian Lara played. In the case of Mark Butcher, his 173 not out against Australia at Headingley in 2001 ranks as one of the very best of the lot. Years of being battered by the Aussies on home soil were swept away on that sunny afternoon as Butch put them to the sword with an innings of sheer brilliance and showed everyone just how good he was. Of course he played several other fine knocks, as befits a man with eight Test tons, but that was the one that stood out and really sealed his place at the top table of the game. When you add the fact that he is an accomplished musician with a band and a brilliant album called Songs from the Sunhouse *(which you should try and get a copy of, by the way) then you realise what a talented bloke this Mr Butcher is.*

MARK BUTCHER – SLEDGE TO MAKE YOU LAUGH

One of the great misconceptions about cricket at the highest level is that it is full of witty sledges and put-downs that have batsmen quivering and fielders rolling in the aisles all day. That simply isn't true.

Firstly, not that much sledging goes on at all these days, largely because teams and players are so focused on the job in hand. If you're worrying about what you're saying to the opposition, then you're not concentrating on doing your bit for the team. Secondly, when there is a bit of chat it is rarely clever or funny. It usually comes under the banner of angry swearing, and that is never going to put someone off – it's water off a duck's back.

What has made sledging such a hot topic are the occasional gems that really do catch everyone's ear and have the desired effect, either of getting a wicket or putting someone down so cleverly that everyone can feel their embarrassment. And, yes, when it comes to sledging the Aussies are pretty good at it.

We've had our fair share of exponents, too, whether it is Freddie Flintoff telling Tino Best to 'Mind the windows' just before the West Indian charged down the wicket and missed the ball, or Ian Botham's reply to Rod Marsh's question 'How's your wife and my kids?' – 'Oh, the missus is fine but the kids are retarded.'

There is a long line of classic sledges through the years, but without question the best I ever came across was a very simple, very funny and very original put-down by Aussie skipper Steve Waugh to his opposite man, Nasser Hussain. On the 2002/03 Ashes tour Down Under, we were playing the last Test at Sydney and England had been battered from pillar to post throughout the trip. Australia hadn't just won the contests out in the middle with bat and ball but they'd won the mental battle, too. The mental disintegration that Steve Waugh always goes on about is sledging pure and simple and his team were very good at it.

Most of the time it was pretty coarse and pretty blunt, but every now and again came these little pearls that made everyone chuckle, even the batsman on the end of it. I was standing at the non-striker's end at the SCG and was batting with Nasser. He'd been given a tough task on this tour, with injuries galore to deal with as well as a rampant Aussie side. But he'd held it together pretty well, and in my opinion came out of that trip with his head held high. He was at the striker's end, battling away with Shane Warne and doing a decent job of keeping the spinner at bay on a tricky pitch.

I should explain that one of Nasser's nicknames is 'Beaky', owing to a side profile that wouldn't look out of place on a puffin. Warne wasn't having much joy so he started talking to Nasser, trying to unsettle him, but it wasn't working. Behind the stumps Adam Gilchrist was chirping away as well, but Nasser was in a bit of a bubble and playing well. At that point Warne turned to his captain, Waugh, at cover and said: 'Hey, skipper, I reckon we should get a catcher right in under his nose.' So Waugh took two steps further away from Nas and said, 'Is this close enough?'

That was it – even Nasser couldn't avoid a chuckle. A schnoz like his is ripe for jokes, but that one was a beauty from Waugh, and as I stood at the non-striker's end next to Warney all you could see were my shoulders bobbing up and down as I tried to suppress my giggles. I failed miserably.

For every player blessed with bundles of talent, there are 10 more who have to work doubly hard to get up to their level. It has always been that way, but if the talented players don't work hard then they will get overtaken by the rest and I can't even begin to think of how many players Paul Collingwood overtook to have a fabulous England career. He squeezed every last drop of ability out of himself and it was easily good enough to be a success at the top level. Always a decent one-day cricketer, Collingwood turned himself into a more than useful Test match batsman and was there for some of England's greatest triumphs, none more so than the Ashes win Down Under. Perhaps his greatest achievement, though, was leading his country to a first ever global tournament victory in the 2012 World Twenty20. Not bad for a lad from the Northeast who took on the world and won.

PAUL COLLINGWOOD – ARMED AND DANGEROUS

By far and away the thing that I will miss most about international cricket is the buzz you get from performing at your best and winning games for your team in front of a big crowd. A full house at Lord's, Chester-le-Street or the Melbourne Cricket Ground gets the juices flowing and that is where you want to be producing your best performances.

Cricket isn't quite like other sports due to the length of time it takes to play it, so the way in which the fans join in is a bit different. Rather than continuous chanting as in football, you tend to get moments of noise when wickets fall or boundaries are scored, until into the afternoon session when enough has been drunk for the singing to get going. That is something you love as an England player – the Barmy Army striking up a tune and singing your name as you bat is one of life's great pleasures.

I think people saw how much I loved it when, in my last Test for England in Sydney, I asked Andrew Strauss, our captain, whether I could go down and field on the boundary in front of them and soak it all up as we were on the verge of an historic series win Down Under. Straussy let me go and I had a ball down there, signing a few autographs, singing a few songs and generally whipping them up into a frenzy. Bill 'the trumpet' Cooper is their musical leader and thankfully he was able to blow his horn to his heart's content, after some debate as to whether he would be able to bring his instrument in with him at all. I think I'm right in saying that he was the only person allowed to bring a musical instrument into the grounds during that series, otherwise there's a complete ban. And there are plenty of other things that aren't allowed either.

Back at home, the England and Wales Cricket Board are also rightly twitchy about what they allow fans to bring into the grounds with them. Gone are the days when punters would flood into The Oval with a case of beer, or a few bottles of wine, for their consumption, along with the odd conch shell to blast as the West Indies racked up run after run. You can still bring in the odd sandwich and newspaper but not a great deal else, and when it comes to ICC global events things can get stricter still – they even confiscated water bottles during the World Twenty20 in the Caribbean.

Cricket in England is not quite like football when it comes to missiles, such as coins, being thrown on to the field of play. The worst thing you have to avoid at Lord's is the flying champagne corks as the well-heeled punters enjoy themselves on a summer's day.

However, the same cannot be said for India. The crowds there are usually good value and they are so excited to see their heroes up close that they go wild for even the smallest acknowledgement. They also like it when the opposition pay them a bit of attention too, but they are not remotely interested in you doing well. We've seen in the past that when their team is struggling they can get a bit restless, as in the World Cup semi-final of 1996 against Sri Lanka.

Still, a few of the England boys got a surprise in 2002 on a one-day tour to India, when we caused a bit of an upset. We were 3–1 down heading into the final two matches of the series and next stop was Delhi. Obviously we needed to win both games to draw the series and those with good memories will recall how we did just that, with Andrew Flintoff playing a starring role. At one stage he whipped off his shirt after a performance he described as 'not bad for a fat lad'.

Anyway, in Delhi we had posted a useful total of 271 for five on the back of a hundred from Nick Knight and we had gone out in the field to defend it. The noise can be deafening at times so it is not always easy to hear what people are saying in the outfield, but there seemed to be yelps coming from Ashley Giles midway through the innings. Gilo was fielding on the boundary at mid-wicket for an over and then would come into the ring rubbing his backside. We watched him go back out to the fence, where he would yell and grab his bum at the same time.

'What's wrong Gilo?' I asked

'There's a bloody sniper in the crowd and he keeps nipping me on my arse!' he replied. At which point he pulled down his trousers and showed me three little red marks on his bum where some kind of pellet had struck him. I must admit I shouldn't have laughed as much as I did, but I did at least tell him to have a word with the umpire.

He was bowling pretty well at the time so he had a chat with the umpire at his end and asked for a bit of advice. The official pretty much shrugged his shoulders and said there was nothing he could do. Gilo went back out into the deep and, sure enough, 'YEEOOOWW!' came the cry as another pellet pinged him. Nasser Hussain was our captain and not the most sympathetic of men, but once he'd stopped laughing he could see the point of saving his bowler from more punishment, so he sent the sub fielder, who happened to be Ben Hollioake, out to field there instead.

A few balls later 'YEEOOOWW!!' cried Ben, who was rubbing his bum and shaking his fist at the crowd. Unsurprisingly that didn't solve the problem. He just inspired the offending pea shooter to keep up the punishment, and each time he turned round he was greeted with the sort of reaction that would delight John Bishop – huge howls of laughter from about 10,000 people.

Poor old Gilo wasn't saved from discomfort, though. He took five for 57 to win the man-of-the-match prize, but every time a wicket fell we all went to congratulate him and the traditional bum pat that signifies 'well done' in cricket was just a pain in the arse for him.

The search for the next Ian Botham began in English cricket before I had even quit the game. That was hardly fair on any young lad trying to make his way, and I've never quite understood why we can't just take players for who they are. The better players and the stronger-minded ones take no notice and just get on with being themselves, and there is no better example than Dominic Cork, who for five years or so was truly world class and should have played far more Test matches than the 37 he was picked for. He was a tough cookie, full of confidence and with the ability to back it up. A genuinely quick outswing bowler, he had a glorious action that allowed him to play the game for as long as he did. Only recently retired, he has finally said goodbye to a game that he clearly loved dearly and was very very good at.

DOMINIC CORK – TAKING CHARGE

When you grow up dreaming of playing cricket for England you never actually think that it will come true. You run around in the back garden pretending to be your heroes and that you are hitting the winning runs in front of a packed house at Lord's. Like so many other players of my generation and beyond, I dreamed of being Ian Botham, taking wickets and smashing sixes for fun. He was the guy we all looked up to and is the hero who's inspired me throughout my cricketing life.

Imagine, then, what it felt like to actually share a dressing room with him on my England debut. As it turned out, it was both my debut and his final match for England, and unbeknown to either of us it was to have a huge impact on my career and in particular on one of my highlights in an England shirt. And the reason had nothing to do with anything he did on the field.

We had all gathered up in Manchester for the final one-day game of summer 1992, against Pakistan at Old Trafford. Chris Lewis had played in the previous matches but was ill and unavailable for this one so they called me up. I was just 20 years old and pretty wide-eyed to the whole thing. People who know me and have played with me will tell you that I'm a confident sort of character; I like to get stuck in and around a cricket team and I've usually got something to say but I can assure you that was *not* the case on my England debut. I was desperate to play well and that probably kept me in check for much of the build-up to the game.

In the dressing room before the match, Mickey Stewart, our coach, was giving one of his team talks. He had written out the names of the Pakistani batsmen on a flipchart and was busy going through the details of how we were to try and get them out. Beefy was sitting the other side of the dressing room, listening to Mickey, and I was sat watching Beefy. Here was my hero, and I was in the same team as him – I couldn't believe it.

Just then, midway through Mickey's talk, Beefy got up and took the pen off him and stood next to the flipchart. He took one look at the names on the board – Aamer Sohail, Ramiz Raja, Inzamam-ul-Haq and other big players – and one by one he put a line through them and each time said, 'Don't worry, I'll get him out. Yep, I'll get him out. I'll get him out . . .' He then turned to Alec Stewart and a couple of our batsmen and said,

'You boys go and get the runs. I'll get his lot out and then we'll have a drink to celebrate.'

He said it so matter-of-factly, there was no hint of doubt in his voice or his manner. And there was no laughing or joking from the rest of the team at what I thought could have just been bravado. He genuinely believed it, and I think plenty in that dressing room believed he could do it, too.

Enough people in there had seen him do enough incredible things on a cricket pitch that they probably thought, why not? I was mesmerised and thought, this is what it means to be an England cricketer.

We went on to win that game and although it was the one and only time I played with him it had a big impact on me, as became clear in a Test at the same ground against the West Indies in 1995.

We were all grouped together in the dressing room before play on day four. Brian Lara and Richie Richardson were the men in the middle and we were struggling to make the break-through. We were still ahead, but with only three wickets down the Windies were moving into position to set us a big total. I had made my Test debut earlier in the series but had been around the squad for a while and felt confident. The ball was coming out well and I just felt like things were going right for me.

The previous day I had scored my first Test fifty despite actu-ally hitting my own wicket in the process. I had played a back-foot shot off Ian Bishop, ran four and then when I stopped I noticed a bail on the floor. I picked it up and put it back on, thinking that the wicket-keeper, Junior Murray, had knocked it off coming up to collect the ball. At that moment Richie appealed, but umpire Dickie Bird told him not to be so stupid. Obviously at the lunch break I realised how lucky I'd been.

So before the fourth day, Mike Atherton, our captain, got us all together and gave an impassioned talk about how someone had to step up and do something, and how the game would slip away from us quickly if we let Brian cut loose. Perhaps it was being in the same dressing room as on my one-day debut, I'm not sure, but I remembered what Beefy had said and stood up and said to Athers, 'I'll do it, I'll get him out. Give me the first over.'

Now, don't get me wrong, I'm not Beefy. But sometimes in cricket, and in sport generally, you've got to at least try to seize the moment. And even though it will go wrong every now and then, sometimes it all comes together and that is why you do what you do.

I came charging in and for the first four balls of that over there was no suggestion anything was happening. Lara picked me off for an easy single, I bowled wide and I bowled a no-ball. But then it happened. Richie left one alone and it deflected off his pad and on to the stumps via his bat. A little lucky maybe. Then, surprisingly, Junior Murray came out ahead of Carl Hooper and I always fancied him as a walking LBW wicket. Full and straight did the trick and he was gone. I think he's still walking back to the pavilion, it was that slow – he'll get there soon!

I should probably give him a bit more credit, because he knew that Carl was in the loo, which is why he came out first. He was probably giving him a bit more time to get out to the middle. When he did, you might think he'd be a little flustered at having to leave the toilet quickly to get out there, but Carl Hooper doesn't do flustered. He was as relaxed as ever, maybe too relaxed as another LBW gave me my hat-trick and put England right on top. Of course Brian Lara was still there and thanks to his 143 we actually still had 94 to get to win the match, which we did.

It was a fantastic moment in my career and a terrific win for England after so much pain at the hands of the Windies in the recent past. Beefy knew all about losing to them throughout the 1980s, but that win had more to do with him than he realises.

If wicket-keepers are madmen and batsmen are boring then spin-ners are definitely the mischievous members of the dressing room. Think Shane Warne, Phil Tufnell and, of course, Robert Croft. Always cheeky, but always thinking, after a lifetime of twirling Glamorgan and England to some memorable victories he has finally decided to call it a day. But he won't stray too far from his beloved Swalec Stadium – he loves it far too much for that and he embodies everything good about it. At a difficult time for English cricket it was always good to see our Welsh chum doing his bit, and if there had been a bit more consistency to selection and a bit more faith in spin, Crofty could have doubled his caps and trebled his Test wick-ets without a hitch. A solid team man who never leaves you without a drink or a laugh.

ROBERT CROFT – WALES RED THROUGH AND THROUGH

Glamorgan were playing at Cambridge one day and it was hammering down with rain, so we were in the dressing room trying to find ways to amuse ourselves. Some of the guys were playing cards, others were reading or just milling about. There was myself and Tony Cottey and we were just mucking about having a laugh, and Hugh Morris was in there as well, tell-ing a few jokes and stuff like that. While he was holding court, talking away to someone else, Tony and I thought it would be funny to rub a little Deep Heat into his underwear because we were still young lads and we were a bit silly.

Anybody who has ever been in a sports changing room will know what Deep Heat is all about. It is a creamy paste that gets rubbed into people's muscles when they're feeling a bit sore or stiff and it helps loosen things up. It absolutely stinks and under no circumstances should it be put anywhere other than on the skin of the sore area because otherwise it just hurts.

There has always been a streak of silliness running through the Glamorgan dressing room and this was just another example, although I'm sure we weren't the first or the last to have a bit of fun with it. We smeared it all over the underside of Hugh's boxer shorts and we then took them outside so as not to draw attention to the smell. A few minutes later the stink had died down so we brought them back in and put them on his hook. We had a bit of a chuckle about it, and waited to see if he would notice. He didn't, and when something else took our attention we actually forgot that we had done it.

It wasn't until later, when we were driving back home, that we noticed Hugh's face in the car behind us getting redder and redder and redder. I described to Tony, who was in the car with me, what I could see through the rear-view mirror and we burst into laughter when we realised what was causing it. At that point he actually stuck his head out the window like an overexcited dog because he was on fire. He could see us turning round and laughing at him, so he clearly let out a stream of invective at us, but as we were driving along his words got lost on the wind and he could have been singing 'Bread of Heaven' for all we knew!

After six hours in the dressing room the underwear didn't really smell much at all so when Hugh put them on he wouldn't have noticed anything. And it turns out that Deep Heat actually reacts to warmth and contact with the skin as opposed to clothing. So it would have needed the length of time it took Hugh to put his clothes on, walk to the car and sit down for it all to get going and have an effect.

Hugh's car finally pulled up alongside ours in some traffic and with his head already out of the window he took full advantage to let us know what he thought. He also took the opportunity to get rid of the offending items from his nether regions. It was quite a display of contortion as he wriggled out of the underwear; unfortunately he couldn't quite get his trousers back on quickly enough to avoid providing a passing cyclist a good eyeful as she made her way home. If Hugh's face wasn't red from the Deep Heat any more it certainly was from the embarrassment.

The silly things men get up to when they are in a sports team, they'd never dream of doing if they were in the normal world. Whether it is Deep Heat in the underwear or snipping the end off someone's socks, they just wouldn't do it.

Saying goodbye to being a professional cricketer was a hugely difficult wrench because it felt like I'd been representing my country for all of it and that is a tough thing to walk away from. I always felt that playing for Glamorgan was like playing for Wales and then when I got the chance to play Test cricket for England, well, that was like playing for the Lions. We've had a few Welsh boys, a few Scots and a few Irishmen playing cricket for England and Test cricket remains the pinnacle of the game. Despite my allegiance to English cricket it doesn't stretch to other sports and back in 2003 I got into a bit of a row with one of my old team-mates because of it.

We were in Sri Lanka during the rugby World Cup and due

to the time differences the final was on at the perfect time of three o'clock on a Saturday afternoon. Luckily for us we weren't playing that day and the Taj Samudra hotel arranged for a giant screen to be placed in the bar so that we could all watch it. Of course, the vast majority watching the game were supporting England, but I just couldn't bring myself to do that. It is not that I wanted Australia to win; I just didn't have much love for either side, and as a fervent Welsh supporter I wasn't about to start cheering for the England rugby team. That would be sacrilegious. So I sat resolutely with arms crossed through-out the game, and while others jumped up and celebrated when Jason Robinson went over for the try I just shrugged my shoulders. And I couldn't help but chuckle with each penalty against England's scrum as Australia clawed their way back into the game.

When the match went into extra time with the scores tied, I made some smart alec comment about Australia prolonging the torture before going on to win it, at which point Angus Fraser, an old England team-mate who was working as a journalist by then, threw a punch at me and told me not to be so unpatriotic. I barely noticed it since Gussy punches like a girl, but he was getting more and more worked up over it.

When the Jonny Wilkinson drop goal went over the whole bar erupted and I must admit I was pretty impressed by what he had done, but I couldn't now show that, so while the rest of the England team were celebrating I stayed out of the way. No big deal, I thought, but Sky Sports News were there filming the players' reactions to the victory. My phone then burst into life as I got bombarded with calls and text messages about my glum expression, when all around there were happy England players celebrating what their rugby counterparts had achieved.

The funny thing was, some of my mates had a go at me for being sour, others (my Welsh mates) thought I was spot on, and a few die-hards thought I wasn't sour enough!

Phil DeFreitas will always get the warmest of welcomes from me after passing the Botham test with flying colours. By which I mean he was my roommate on his first tour to Australia in 1986/87 and for two weeks before the family came out he held firm and was as good a roomie as anyone would want. He was great company in between matches and training sessions, he was a willing participant in the more sociable aspects of touring life, and he was keen to learn as much as he could about bowling in international cricket. For a 20-year-old lad, that was perfect. He could have retreated into his shell sharing a room with me, but he was great fun and a high-quality cricketer to go with it. Although he didn't have a classical action, he was a classic English swing bowler with tremendous control of a ball when it started to move. He probably deserved a few more than the 140 Test wickets he took for England, but when you're dropped and recalled as many times as he was (15 times by the way) it is hard to get into the sort of form that continuity in the team brings you. Still, he was a class act throughout his career. Playing first-class cricket into his 40th year shows just how good he was and by the time he finished there was no question that he had squeezed every last drop of cricket out of himself.

PHIL DeFREITAS – PRANKSTER EXTRAORDINAIRE

For all the cricket that you play as a professional – and there is an awful lot – the nature of the game means you always have a fair bit of time on your hands, especially if you're a bowler. If you're a half-decent batsman, you could be involved in the game from start to finish, but if you're a quickie like I was then the end of the opposition innings was always followed by a decent break, especially if your batters are in form.

So what do you do if, like I was, you're young, love dressing-room banter and are a born joker? You get stuck into all the pranks and high jinks going on and have a jolly good time. Nearly every practical joke that has been played on me and I have played on others has been taken well. It is all part and parcel of dressing-room life, although on one or two occasions it might have spilt over.

Back when I first played for Leicestershire there was an incident that followed me around – much like a similar thing followed Kevin Pietersen after his time at Nottinghamshire – namely, when Jonathan Agnew launched my kit off the dressing-room balcony and all over the bemused public below. It just so happened that my V12 bat almost decapitated the cricket journalist who was there covering the game at the time, so there was no chance of keeping it quiet.

I used to travel to games with a fellow young player, Phil Whitticase, while Aggers and Peter Willey, the two senior men in the Leicestershire side, would travel together. It was in the days when the younger players had to do various jobs, like whiten the boots of the senior players, and because Phil and I were two of the young pups, Aggers and Peter used to take the mickey out of us.

One day we were travelling back from somewhere like New Road and as a bit of a joke Phil and I put a banana up the exhaust pipe of their car and watched it splutter and shudder its way around the car park before conking out. We got a right telling-off from them as a result so the only response was to up the ante.

We got back to Grace Road and Aggers was feeling a little under the weather, so the chef had made him a special meal. He came and sat down next to me and was about to get stuck in. There was only a brief chance for me, but I managed to loosen the lid of the salt cellar enough so that when he used it the whole contents poured over his meal. It was a classic cricket prank, but on this occasion Aggers didn't take too kindly to it at all. In fact, he lost it completely and stormed up to the dressing room and proceeded to throw all my kit over the balcony. The thing about that incident is that most people thought Aggers and I hated each other because of it, but actually that wasn't true at all. There was a healthy dose of respect between us and it really was just an escalating series of wind-ups and retaliations, but we soon got over it and we're firm friends to this day.

At Derbyshire I met up with another massive prankster by the name of Colin Wells and he was the man who introduced me to the wonderful world of Super Glue. He did this by waiting for the moment when, following play one day, there was a meet-and-greet for some important guests of the club in the corporate hospitality area. We all had to get our suits and ties on, and of course our best shoes. Leaving the dressing room, all I could hear was the tap tap tap of a dancer's shoes as I walked. I thought I must have stepped on a tack or something, but it was unusually loud. As I walked a bit more I knew I had to sort it out, so I took off my shoes and discovered about six penny coins Super Glued to the soles. I had no chance of getting them off in time, so I had to walk upstairs making a clatter and then once I was in the room, try and stay as still as possible. What really got me, though, was that when I actually tried to take them off, I wrecked my shoes and had to get them re-soled at the cobblers.

By far the best prank that I've ever played was with my old partner in crime at Derbyshire, Dominic Cork. We were down at Lord's in 1995 and in a rain-affected match things were meandering towards a draw, so we had a fair bit of time on our hands. The third day was actually washed out completely and it was while we were hanging around that Corky and I had an idea. We had the great South African batsman Daryll Cullinan as our overseas player that year and, although he was a great lad, he could also be a bit fiery.

When you play at Lord's you park behind the pavilion in what's known as car park No. 6. During the long break for rain, Corky and I decide we are going to move Daryll's swanky Mercedes. We nick his keys out of his pocket, drive his car to the nursery ground, only about 700 metres away but far enough, and then return the keys to his pocket.

Eventually play is called off for the day and we start to head back to the hotel. We get to the car park and Daryll is going absolutely mental because someone has nicked his car.

The officials at the MCC get a right old ear-bashing as Daryll questions their security and demands to know what has happened. They try to tell him that it must be some kind of mistake, there must be a simple explanation, but he's having none of it. He gets a lift back to the hotel and is about to ring the police when Corky and I think it is probably time to own up, and when we do he goes even more berserk than before.

He flew into an almighty rage and told us to leave his private possessions alone, with a few expletives thrown in for good measure. I don't think it helped that we just stood there laughing at him. With the vein in his neck about to burst he demanded that we go back and get his car because he needed it to go out that evening. The prank had worked so well, and his face was such a picture when we told him, that we decided to go and get the car to avoid any irreversible fallout. The only problem was that by the time we got back to the ground the gates were shut and we couldn't get in. Fearing another bollocking from Daryll, Corky did well to think on his feet and suggest we give Mick Hunt, the groundsman, a call to see if he'd let us in. Thankfully he obliged, and when he heard the story, he just turned around muttering something about 'two prats' as he went to check on his pitch.

DIGGING UP A PRING
IN THE CAR PARK

I have a confession to make: I like a drink.

Okay, so that isn't exactly the most earth-shattering news. In fact, during my playing days you would have to look long and hard and far to find a player who didn't like to unwind with a drink or two after a hard day out in the field. It was part and parcel of the game, and it was certainly part of the fun of the sporting environment in which you played hard and celebrated just as hard afterwards. I'm glad to see that for all the changes the game has gone through, a few beers with your mates after the job has been done is still as much a part of the fabric as ever.

What has definitely changed is the amount the players get through, especially mid-match. There is a lot more care over what goes into their bodies full stop and alcohol is much more tightly regulated than it was in my time. This is as true of the county game as it is of international cricket, so some of the mischief we used to get up to at Somerset and then Worcestershire is far less likely to happen – although I hear there is still room for releasing a bit of pressure if you're not too careless.

The question is how far do you go? Just as important for a cricketer used to be knowing how much you could drink in a given situation and what your limit was if you had to turn up for training or even a match the next day. At the back end of 1987 I was privy to a classic case of misjudgement and even though I played my part these were grown men who should have known better!

The game was between Essex and Worcestershire and it happened to be our final away game of the season. As was the tradition of the time, the season's fines would normally be spent on a night out with the team at the last away game, so I knew I had to be there for that. Unfortunately I was injured; my back was playing havoc and causing me all sorts of problems and I ended up having surgery the following summer, but on this occasion I was just an injured member of the squad. I travelled with the team to Colchester and was keen to support them, although we were effectively playing for pride at that stage.

I knew we would have a good time with the Essex lads. Earlier in the season we'd had a terrific night out in Worcester when Eric Clapton, who'd been spending a bit of time with me, put on an impromptu gig one evening. So I knew the Essex boys would be up for a bit of fun.

The first day was a washout. The forecast was miserable for the whole game in fact, but the players still had to hang around until the umpires told them there would be no play.

I wasn't playing so I didn't need to hang around. I told the boys to meet me in a pub later that evening when they were let off the hook. Eventually they all showed up and, seeing as I was in charge of the fines kitty, I was the man in the chair at the bar. There was a nice atmosphere to the place, the drinks started to flow and everyone was having a good time.

After a few rounds, several players from both sides made their excuses and left, while I kept the drinks coming. There was a fair bit of chat among the lads about the weather, how the rain wasn't going anywhere and the chances of playing the next day were remote at best. Still, it is always a bit of a gamble to assume there will be no play. The only cricketer at the bar who knew for sure he wouldn't be playing the next day was yours truly, and I fancied a tequila. Those who know a bit about my charity walks will recall that my drink of choice for the particularly tough parts is a tequila-based rocket fuel. On this night, it was straight and just for fun.

Joining me in the tasting session were two other players, Derek Pringle from Essex and Phil Weston from Worcestershire, plus an old friend of Pring's called Winston Bynorth, who is a rather brilliant photographer, and they didn't hold back. I lined up the tequilas and they saw them away, with a little help from me of course.

Now, it is not for me to say when someone has had too much, but when I spotted Pring passed out between two cars in the car park, I did wonder whether he had reached his limit. Together with Winston we managed to help him up and into a cab to take him to his mother's house, which was nearby.

I thought nothing more of it as I headed back to the hotel, happy after a fun evening. The next day I made it to the ground reasonably early, and thankfully I've never really been one to suffer from hangovers. A couple of Red Bulls – or in those days a coffee and some water – and I was fine. In any case, you've just got to get on with it. Unfortunately for Pring, his way of getting on with it was to simply roll over and keep snoozing.

He hadn't turned up at the ground and, lo and behold, conditions were just fine for cricket and play was going to start on time. The two captains went out for the toss and there was still no sign of him, at which point there was speculation about where he might have cracked on to after the pub. I reassured everyone that he most certainly hadn't gone anywhere else after the pub, but I didn't reveal that it was because he had been lying face down in a car park.

At 10.40 the Essex club secretary thought it prudent to put a call into his mother's place and enquire as to his whereabouts. 'Are you planning on playing today, Derek?' he asked, to which the expletive-laden response revealed he was on his way.

Apparently Pring shot out of bed, with his mate Winston looking on and chuckling to himself at his misfortune – having had no intention of waking him up, I might add. When he got to the ground his heart sank because it became clear that Essex were in the field because the boys were making their way out. As he ran into the pavilion to get changed, Keith Fletcher shouted at Graham Gooch, the captain: 'Oi, Goochie, make him bowl all day!!'

I just laughed and told him to get those bowling boots on and roll up his sleeves. In our dressing room was Phil, who couldn't have been happier. He was a touch late himself and, just before the toss, was praying our captain would win it and bat first, so when the news came back that Essex had won the toss his worst fears were about to be realised. Until it was followed up with '. . . and they're fielding'. 'Oh yes! There is a God!' he exclaimed. There was no divine intervention for Pring, who spent the day sweating tequila out of his pores, while Phil had a lovely kip in the corner of the dressing room.

I didn't really know what all the fuss was about; it was only a few drinks and, in fact, I went out again that night. The other two didn't.

The travelling press pack is an integral part of the international touring scene and thankfully the players and the cricket press have usually got on pretty well. These are not the journos you have to worry about. They only care about whether you've won or lost or scored runs or taken wickets. When they give you a bit of a serve, it is normally because you deserve it. A stalwart of these trips is John Etheridge, who was covering England tours when I was playing and is still doing it now to his normal high standards. People think that to write for the tabloids, and the Sun in particular, doesn't take a great deal of thought or effort, when actually it is harder to condense the same information into a smaller space, and be witty with it as well. John has done this with class and ability for years and is a master of his trade. He is also a good man to spend a few hours with in a bar, putting the world to rights.

JOHN ETHERIDGE – HACKING ROUND THE GOLF COURSE

By covering the England cricket team at home and abroad for more than 20 years for the old 'currant bun' – the *Sun* – I have seen my fair share of scrapes, japes and mishaps on and off the cricket field, and that is just in the press corps.

Touring with England is a particular pleasure and, while we might not be scoring runs or taking wickets, we have a lot in common with the players in terms of our circumstances: being away from home and family for long periods, and trying to find a sense of community and comradeship often with people who are effectively your rivals. So you find things to do on tour to take your mind off things, whether it is visiting a tourist attraction or a nice local restaurant, or doing a spot of activity like golf.

During the 1997 one-day tour to Sharjah, there was an opportunity to play some golf in nearby Dubai and we were only too glad to take it. The course was called Dubai Creek and having visited it again recently it remains a rather magnificent facility. Back then the golf club was a gem in a place that hadn't quite got into the rapid development that characterises it now. It had all the mod cons you'd expect from a top-level course, with buggies mandatory in the searing heat. And the heat is something that certainly hasn't changed.

On the 12th hole I teed off and went looking for my ball. I spotted it in a little hollow, so parked up and trotted down towards it, with five iron in hand. Fully focused on the ball and the shot I needed to play, I looked up for the flag and then back down at the ball. I did it a second time. Just then I heard what could only be described as a gentle rumble behind me; it was enough to take my attention and, turning round, I was transfixed as I watched my golf buggy trundle down the slope up to a gentle lip, take off into the air and land solidly into . . . Dubai Creek. I clearly hadn't depressed the brake fully and the slope was just enough for it to get up a real head of steam. There was no way of stopping it, especially when I could only watch it happen, frozen in horror.

The depth of the water happened to be exactly the same as the height of the golf cart, so within moments all you could see was the white top of the buggy and various small items as they rose to the surface. Wallets, mobile phones and golf tees. I was understandably mortified. My colleagues were understandably in stitches. The young caddies and workers on the course all thought it was rather funny too, but at least they did something about it, stripping off and diving for clubs and other items. They fished them out and I've still got the rusted items at home. It was a saltwater creek, so the damage was done to my golf clubs as well as my pride.

As for the buggy, the benefit of having so much construction work going on in the area was that it didn't take long to source a forklift truck, which was able to pull it out of the water with ropes and a bit of ingenuity. I was suitably apologetic and embarrassed but was given reassurances that it happened all the time. I wasn't sure about that, but I took them at their word and thought nothing more of it.

Imagine my surprise when a couple of days later I received a letter demanding payment for their ruined golf buggy, citing my reckless behaviour. On the advice of my fellow journalist, golf player and former England cricketer, Mike Selvey, and David Facey, another journo, I made a grovelling phone call to the golf club to see whether we might be able to reach some kind of understanding. They reassured me again that it was not a problem, that it had happened before.

'But what about the stern letter you sent me?' I enquired.

'What letter?' came the response, as it dawned on me that I'd been had by my fellow writers good and proper.

Years later there would be no such calamity on another golf day, this time in the Caribbean during the World Twenty20. This was a day on which the glamour and cachet that people associate with the job actually occurred. Trust me, it is not normally like this.

As a guest of Johnnie Walker, the official drink for West Indies cricket, I was invited to play a round at the newly installed Apes Hill golf course in Barbados, and joining me was Alan Wilkins, the former Glamorgan and Gloucestershire cricketer and now well-respected TV presenter and commentator, plus two others you might have heard of – Sir Garfield Sobers and SIR Vivian Richards, two of the greatest batsmen the game has seen and both pretty handy with a golf club, too.

Up on the first tee, with everyone watching and bristling with excitement, the three aforementioned players drive their balls off into the sunset and down the fairway. Yours truly steps up, takes a couple of practice swings and then addresses the ball. Club head is pulled back and then with an almighty whoosh it comes down and I look off into the distance for the ball. It remains at my feet. I ignore the sniggering and try again. This time I make a connection and the ball flies off down the fairway, but veering wildly right and into the long rough.

I head off to look for it, and although I haven't asked them to, so do the Sirs. I look up and I've got two blokes with more than 16,000 Test runs between them scratching around in the dirt looking for my ball. It is a surreal moment. Viv finds it and points it out to me. 'Thanks, Viv,' I say. 'After years of sending Englishmen to go and look for the ball after you've hit it, I suppose it was about time the boot was on the other foot and you had to look for one of ours!'

He glared at me, that same stare that has sent shivers down many a bowler's spine, and then he broke into a smile before reminding me, 'And it will be the last time.' I wasn't about to argue and thankfully the rest of the round went off without any more embarrassment.

Talking of which, I'm not sure who was more embarrassed on a tour to South Africa in 1995, me or John Edrich. The former England batsman was there as the batting coach with Ray Illingworth's team and managed unintentionally to intercept a message meant for me. It was sent by my wife Cristina, who is Spanish, and it just so happens that my nickname for her is Inny. The faxed letter was written with the normal love and affection you would expect between a husband and wife, and was topped and tailed with 'Dear John' and 'Lots of love, Inny'.

Now, to the untrained eye scanning my wife's handwriting, it is possible to read 'Inny' as 'Illy', so when the hotel staff delivered this letter to John Edrich rather than John Etheridge, you could see why the England management had an awkward day not knowing quite how to discuss the feelings that Ray Illingworth clearly had for John Edrich!

The great thing about sport is that there will always be someone on the conveyor belt, about to replace those who are there. We think that such and such a player can never be replaced or that there will never be another like so-and-so. Nonsense. And every once in a while someone bursts on to the scene and does something remarkable. Steve Finn is a bowler in that bracket. By taking 50 Test match wickets by the age of 22 years and 63 days, he became the youngest Englishman to get to that landmark, and I thought it was about time someone took that record off me. He's a diligent, dedicated pace bowler with a little something extra. A bit more height than most, a bit more pace too, and a willingness to keep bowling no matter how tough it is. A good man to have in your team.

STEVEN FINN –
IMPRESSING THE BOSS

Even though I made my England debut only fairly recently, people involved in and around my club all seem to think that it was my fellow Middlesex man, Andrew Strauss, who gave me my first cap. They think it's lovely that a well-respected legend of the club like Straussy got to be the one to dish out caps to other younger players coming through at Lord's.

Eoin Morgan had enjoyed this experience, but I was given my cap by Alastair Cook because I'd been called up – rather unexpectedly – for a one-Test series when Straussy was being rested. And, as I now tell people, if Straussy had been captain he might not have picked me after what I did to him as a 14-year-old.

It was back in 2004 and I was taking part in winter training with the Middlesex academy in our indoor school at Finchley, north London. For those of you who have not spent the odd winter's evening training there, it is a mix between Old Trafford, The Oval and Perth. It is quick.

One day I was bowling with the academy under the watchful eye of Jason Pooley, who was the second-team coach at the time and a former Middlesex batsman. Jase is a top bloke and undoubtedly has the gift of the gab. Midway through our session Straussy came in and asked Jason if we would mind bowling to him because he wanted to have a net. I had never met him before and was a little bit in awe. He was a senior player at the club, he had captained the side and had already played one-day cricket for England. At that stage he had just returned from the tour to the West Indies but hadn't played in the Tests. As we all now know, later that summer he made his Test debut at Lord's, scored a hundred and went on to have a fabulous international career.

Still, here I was, this scrawny 14-year-old running in to bowl to a future England captain. He was very polite beforehand and then he went to work. He slapped me everywhere, anything slightly short of a length was cut viciously and with real power and for the first time it made me realise just how good players were at his level.

I kept bowling and then, out of nowhere, I released a pretty quick ball which dropped just a fraction shorter than I wanted and, this being Finchley, it reared up at Straussy and nearly took his head off. He reeled back, lost his balance and fell over, just when Jase happened to be paying full attention.

'HA! HA! HA! You mug! You've just been put on your arse by a fourteen-year-old!!' said Pooley in his strongest London accent.

'How d'ya feel, superstar! A fourteen-year-old! Wait till I tell the boys about this!'

To which Straussy gave his own sweary response, but somehow it still sounded quite eloquent. I didn't know what he would say to me when he came out of the net, but he was good as gold.

It wasn't until late in 2007 that we first played together for Middlesex, when he came back from England duty, and he was brilliant in the dressing room. I learnt a lot just from watching him and listening to what he had to say about the game, and then when we went out on to the field he gave me one of my best memories. It was a promotion/relegation play-off against Northants at Southgate in the Pro40 League, so it was an important game, and beforehand everyone was talking about starting well and getting into them. I opened the bowling and they sent in Nicky Boje up the order to get on with things. I bowled one to him that he cut with such force that I knew it was four immediately, but somehow Straussy leapt like a salmon and caught it one-handed high above his head. It was an incredible catch and it was my first of three wickets in a game we won and I got my first man-of-the-match award.

I was on my way as a cricketer and I guess you could say it culminated in my Test debut in March 2010, but if it wasn't for my mum I might not have got the chance. I had just arrived home following a tour to the UAE with the England Performance Programme, which had gone pretty well for me. I'd bowled with good rhythm and taken a few wickets, so I thought it would set me up nicely for a full season of bowling with Middlesex as I continued to try and press for international honours.

I must confess I didn't really have a clue what was going on in Bangladesh on the full England tour so I didn't know that they were having a few injury issues. Stuart Broad was having problems with his back, as was Graham Onions, so when he was sent home and they needed a replacement I had no idea that they wanted to call someone up, let alone that the person would be me.

I was at home in bed when my phone went and it was a number I didn't recognise, so I red-buttoned it. It rang again and I ignored it again. When it rang a third time I didn't even bother looking at it and rolled over. I had never spoken to Hugh Morris, the managing director of England cricket, before so I didn't know it was his number. Five minutes later the home phone went, and I thought, I'd better answer that because it will either be for my parents or it will be my parents. It was Mum. 'Steven, what are you doing? Why won't you pick up the bloody phone to Hugh Morris?! He's been trying to call you – now, will you answer your phone!'

Just then it rang and I picked it up, to be told that I was needed to join the squad in Bangladesh and I had a flight that evening. I got my stuff together and arrived in Chittagong the day before the warm-up match. I had been bowling recently in Dubai, so I felt good, and went straight into the game and performed pretty well.

The only downside was that it was very hot and I didn't quite get enough fluids into me, because that evening I started to cramp up. I was lying down on the bed, and meeting several of the England players for the first time. They were all really good to me, but every couple of minutes I would scream out in agony as part of my leg would seize up. I would then stretch out the calf only for the shin to cramp up, and then my arm and then my other leg. It was torture, but the lads found it very amusing.

'Hi, I'm Kevin Pietersen, great to meet you Finny.'

'Hi, Kevin, do you mind if I call you KPEEEEEEEEEEEE!!!!!'

It was highly embarrassing, but thankfully Cooky saw past it and handed me my first Test cap a few days later.

One of the great things about sport, and cricket in particular, is that it is welcoming of every type of person no matter who they are or where they come from, and that variety makes for interesting dressing rooms. Matthew Fleming was as proper an English gent as ever played the game. Eton and the army shaped him, and the nickname 'Jazzer' seems appropriate, but on the cricket field he was as competitive as they come. A tremendous servant to Kent cricket and unlucky not to play more than 11 one-dayers for England, he was wholehearted in everything he did on the field and always looked like he was enjoying himself. Since retiring he's carved out a tremendously successful career in the City, but has remained committed to cricket and is doing his bit in the English game and indeed around the world as an MCC administrator.

MATTHEW FLEMING – SHIP-SHAPE AND BRISTOL FASHION

Cricket has been wonderful to me and has given me some of the happiest memories of my life, both on and off the field, and one of the great things about the game is the friendships you get to make that will last a lifetime. At Kent and with England I was lucky enough to play with Mark Ealham, who was a fantastic cricketer and an even better mate. However, like all good, lengthy close relationships we have had our ups and downs, and occasionally others have seen this close at hand.

Back in 1997 England's one-day team were gearing up for a tournament in Sharjah under Adam Hollioake and both Mark and myself were picked for the tour. I'd had a good summer and thought I might get a sniff of England honours, but hadn't really expected to make the team, while Ealy was already a fixture in the side. Thankfully, we were both called up to the squad and set off on what turned out to be a rather successful and enjoyable trip.

The squad had quite a few good tourists in it, guys like Dougie Brown, Ashley Giles and the captain 'Smokey' were great lads and made the most of the trip. The tournament was between us, the West Indies, India and Pakistan, and, as it was being held in the Middle East, the two subcontinent teams were the favourites to get to the final. For whatever reason they didn't quite play to their full potential, while we played a reasonable amount of decent cricket, which meant that it was left to us and the Windies to contest the final.

The way the fixtures fell gave us a couple of extra days off before that game, so one afternoon I decided to relax by the pool with a good book. I was on one of those comfortable sun loungers and must have nodded off in the sunshine because the next thing I knew I was being tipped up and rolled towards the water.

I quickly surmised that there was very little I could do to avoid my watery appointment, so with true style and distinction I slid elegantly into the pool – much to the amusement of my tippee, a certain Mark Alan Ealham – making sure to hold the book high above my head to prevent it from getting wet. I was left to cough and splutter my way out of the pool, swearing my revenge, while all around me had a laugh at my expense.

The next day I managed to persuade the hotel maid to give me the key to Mark's room. I sneaked in and stole his tour trousers, the smart ones that we used to fly in and wear to official functions. I should point out that Mark was and is an incredibly vain man when it comes to his appearance. Always immaculately turned out, not a single hair out of place and just exceptionally organised with his attire.

I took his trousers and went to a tailor in the old part of Sharjah and had them taken up by 12 inches, but leaving in place the little turn-ups at the bottom. I returned to the hotel and to his room, placed them back on the hanger in his wardrobe and left without anyone, bar the maid of course, knowing I had been there.

The next day we played our final and won. Cue celebrations all round. No one gave any thought to the fact that we had a rather early trip to the airport for our flight home. At five the following morning, we were all in the lobby feeling slightly worse for wear, waiting for Mark to come down so we could get on the bus. At that point Mark emerged from the lift looking immaculate from his head to his mid-calf, and to this day it still makes me laugh just thinking about it. He could have been the third Krankie.

What made it all the funnier was that he and his father Alan, the former cricketer, had a total sense of humour failure about the whole thing and for the entire trip home were in a sulk. We had been in the same dressing room for all of our cricketing lives, so knew each other inside out, and he wasn't usually a man to play pranks on. He was a very earnest and conscientious cricketer, and always prepared meticulously and made sure to look his best. As a result he got left alone a little bit in the dressing room when it came to practical jokes, but by that stage I was senior enough to get away with it.

Ian Botham

That period was a nice time because we had done unexpectedly well, the guys on that trip were great fun and the banter flowed endlessly. I always look back on it very fondly – and with a smile at Ealy's short trousers.

Graeme 'Foxy' Fowler is as good a friend as I've made in the game. He and I might have been born hundreds of miles apart, but we've ended up in the right place in the Northeast. He shares my passion for the fun in life and he doesn't take himself too seriously. He was a bloody good cricketer, whose only misfortune was to play the game in Graham Gooch's era. There aren't too many blokes who only play one more Test match after scoring a double century. Since retiring Foxy has shown himself to be a high-quality cricket coach, bringing through cricketers like Andrew Strauss at Durham University while also lending his voice to Test Match Special *for a few years. It is just a shame that his Lancashire lilt can't be heard on those broadcasts anymore.*

GRAEME FOWLER – ALERT AS A FOX

In sport, there are so many legendary stories about legendary players. Sometimes I wonder just how true they are. There are occasions when the event does happen, but not to the person they say; and others when it never took place at all. Beefy Botham is one of those men who has had plenty said and written about him, and not all of it is true. This story is, and it means a lot to me personally.

It was an England v Australia Test match at Adelaide on the 1982/83 Ashes tour. We weren't playing very well: we drew the first Test, lost the second and this was the third in a five-match series so we couldn't afford to lose it.

I was 37 not out overnight, and after three days we were battling to save the match and in effect keep the series alive. I was getting ready to bat and unusually the dressing room was empty bar myself and Beefy. I don't know where everyone else was, but there were just the two of us. He came over to me and said, 'Come on, Fox, you can do this. You can bat all day. If you do that, we'll save this game. Come on, you know you can do it.'

It was only my third Test match and for some reason – probably naivety – I turned to Beefy and said, 'Bat all day?! Who do you think I am, Geoff Boycott? I'm just a lad from Accrington, I'm not some superstar.'

At this point his eyes glazed over, he grabbed me by the shirt collar, pushed me into the wall and leaned in very close to my face and said, 'And how do you think I f**king started?'

He put me down, said nothing more and walked off. I was then left completely alone in the dressing room. I sat down and mulled over what had just happened and, like a clearing of the clouds, I thought, He's right. He's absolutely right. It made me realise that everyone has to start somewhere and why not a match-saving knock in Adelaide for me?

With play about to get underway, I joined David Gower and we walked out to bat 132 runs behind, with nine wickets in hand and two days left to play in the game. I glanced over at Beefy, who just gave me a knowing look, and I felt full of confidence, as if I could take on the world. This was going to be my day.

I returned to the pavilion with the team 132 runs behind, eight wickets in hand and two days left to play!

Needless to say, we lost by eight wickets and that Ashes series was over for us. It remains a special game for me, though, because of what happened with Beefy. People might not remember but I had gone from playing in the Lancashire second XI to playing Test cricket in only 18 months. I didn't really know what was going on. I hadn't thought too much about where I was or what I was doing; we didn't have a coach, let alone the team of support staff the players have now. You were pretty much on your own, and you just picked things up from the senior players. So even though it might not have worked immediately, Beefy's intervention was a huge light-bulb moment in my career and, without it, I might not have scored the runs I went on to make for England.

There were some great guys playing for England during my time with the side and, in a different way, Mike Gatting offered me some support at a vital moment. In 1985, during a Test match against India in Madras, we were coming to the close of the second day and, having batted all day, I was 149 not out with Gatt at the other end.

It had been roasting hot and I was feeling it, but I'd made it through to the last over and it was Ravi Shastri bowling his left-arm spin. The first ball was delivered and Gatt got down on one knee and swept it out towards the boundary fielder. The ball was trickling out there, the fielder was walking in to pick it up, it was the easiest, longest single available to a batsman. I started to walk down the wicket for the single but Gatt hasn't moved.

I'm halfway down the track before I call out, 'Gatt!'

'What?!' comes the reply.

'Don't you want a single?' I ask, as the fielder gathers the ball. For some reason we're having a mid-pitch conversation while the ball is live.

'Look, you've done enough today, get back up the other end and I'll deal with this over and take us to the close.'

There were four men round the bat, in the middle of a Test match, lots of pressure and noise, and yet he told me to stay put. That was an incredibly selfless thing to do. I went back up to the non-striker's end, put my bat between my legs, rested my arms on it and tucked my cap down with head bowed. I didn't back up or anything; all I did was look up when I heard the bowler's footsteps get to the crease and then look back down again and close my eyes. I've got five balls to count and then we're off.

I managed to count three before falling asleep, standing upright in the middle of a Test match! The next thing I heard was the umpire calling, 'Over, and time!'

Rather than walking off, Gatt was striding up the wicket towards me, having realised that I'd nodded off at the crease. We set off back to the pavilion and got the usual back-slapping and congratulations from the lads. It wouldn't happen these days but the first drink they put in my hands was a bottle of beer. I'd been out in that heat for more than six hours, sweated buckets running up and down, so by the time I'd had four mouthfuls of beer I was pissed. In 1985 we didn't know much about rehydration.

On top of this, I'd also grazed my knees diving around in the field beforehand, and because of the various fertilisers they put on the grass the wounds had become infected. So when I got back to the changing room I had bandages stuck to my septic knees, my trousers stuck to the bandages and my pads stuck to my trousers. Each layer had to be literally peeled off me. That evening I was wandering around the hotel with bandages on my knees, in my underwear, beer in hand, pissed as you like and looking like an orphan schoolboy from *Oliver Twist*.

To finish off this tale, the next day I went back out and carried on batting and managed to get my double hundred. When I was eventually out, I was a little surprised to walk past Allan Lamb as he came out to bat. Normally it should have been David Gower to bat next. The press hailed it as a smart bit of tactical captaincy from Gower to push Lamby up the order to get on with things. It was nothing of the sort.

David had been waiting so long with his pads on that he needed to sit down and use the toilet. When I got out David was on the loo, someone rushed to get him, but in the intervening time, sensing there were runs to be had, Lamby grabbed his chance and rushed out ahead of him. David could only watch on and do his trousers up as his team-mate went out and scored his runs, all 62 of them.

KITTING OUT THE WIFE

It takes all sorts to make up a dressing room and that is one of the things that makes cricket such a welcoming parish. You've got your tough guys, your quiet guys, your loud and annoying guys, and in every team there is an eccentric bloke who just does things a bit differently. I've played with plenty of those down the years but the two who stand out are Derek Randall, known as 'Arkle', and Jack Russell. These two simply did things their own way and you just had to stand back and let them get on with it.

I can understand it with Jack because wicket-keepers are mad full stop, but Arkle was in a league of his own when it came to odd behaviour. Rabbiting away to himself and the opposition, he would drive them mad. Not because he was sledging them, but because he just wanted to chat. He would talk about the weather, food, family, anything, just to interact, and they just wanted him to shut up. Sometimes so did we, but you couldn't keep a lid on Arkle.

For all his foibles and idiosyncrasies Arkle was great fun too, and we had plenty of laughs in between some of his special performances for England. The one that sticks out in my mind was back in 1982 on tour to Australia when, under Bob Willis, we were having a bit of a tough old time. Just because things are a little miserable on the field doesn't mean they have to be quite so miserable off it, so following the eight-wicket defeat in Adelaide a few of us decided to drown our sorrows in the hotel bar.

The whole team started out having a few drinks and, as one or two drifted away, there was a group of about six of us left. We had moved on to a lovely little combination of whisky and ice cream, with a bit of soda, I think, thrown in too. Ever the economist, I pointed out that the best way to order these drinks was by the jugful rather than individually. It meant for a rather messy evening.

Midway through, we got chatting to a couple of ladies who had been at the bar and they were game enough to drink what we were drinking. Somehow the conversation turned into a bit of a competition, and at one point Arkle came out with the comment that women had it easy when it came to picking up blokes and that if he dressed up like a woman he wouldn't have any trouble. Well, that was a challenge right there. We arranged for him to swap outfits with one of the ladies and sent him out to see whether he could get picked up.

He certainly did, getting into a truck with a bloke who, we later found out, he thought was in on the joke. We didn't see him for another hour and if we weren't so happy with our whisky and ice cream we might have got worried. Eventually he returned, looking a little flustered. When asked what had happened, he said that some 'cheeky Aussie' had taken him up the road in his truck for a laugh and he thought he would bring him back straight away. He didn't. He took poor Arkle to a secluded spot and tried it on! This came as a big surprise to our middle-order batsman, who revealed: 'I had to get away from him – so I hit him with me handbag!'

He passed the offending weapon back to the lady it belonged to and sat down for a well-deserved recovery drink.

He could play a bit, mind you. I can remember going to visit him at home one spring and being greeted at the door by him wearing a set of cricket pads. 'Just breaking them in, Beefy,' he told me. That was all well and good; slightly different, but fair enough. What I didn't expect to see as we went into the kitchen was Mrs Randall washing up at the sink wearing another pair of her husband's pads, doing the same thing!

That is what reminded me of Jack because he used to get his missus to work on his kit just like Arkle did. In fact, Jack would only let his missus work on his tattered old sun hat, which he wore for his entire career. He would get her to add bits of flannel here and there as it got worn, and she was the only person allowed to wash it before sticking it on a biscuit jar, over a tea cosy and a tea towel, in the airing cupboard to make it just right.

Jack was so particular about the way he wanted things done, a case in point being his Weetabix, which he insisted on having at lunch and tea if he was keeping wicket. He wanted them soaked in milk for precisely 12 minutes, so the 12th man would have to get them ready 10 minutes before the break to make sure they weren't too crispy or too soggy when Jack got off!

Anyway, his hat was one of his most prized possessions, along with his gloves, but on a tour to the Caribbean his culinary skills got the better of him and his hat. After training and back in the hotel suite he was sharing with Graeme Hick, the pair of them were relaxing and getting the session out of their system. Jack wanted to dry his hat, but rather than leave it out in the sun, which would have been the sensible thing to do, he didn't want it to get nicked so he brought it inside. Why anyone would want to steal his old hat was beyond me, but anyway . . .

He brought it inside and in the little kitchenette they had there was an oven. Jack thought he could leave it in there for 20 minutes and it would be dry. Not quite appreciating just how hot ovens can be, he cranked it up, put his hat in and left it. It didn't take long for smoke to fill the apartment. Graeme called out to Jack and asked him if he was cooking anything exciting. 'Don't worry about it, mate, it's just my hat,' came the reply.

'Well, it's burnt.'

At which point Jack ran to the kitchen through the smoke and grabbed his hat. Unsurprisingly, it was too hot to handle and he dropped it to the floor. The hat simply disintegrated. Cue much laughter from Graeme and a few other England players he'd brought to the room. All that was left was the brim. Jack used his one spare hat for the rest of the trip and then got his missus to add the old brim.

Each to their own.

There is a programme on television called Grumpy Old Men. *A load of famous old boys past their best moaning about things not being the way they used to be. That's not for me. But someone who was born to be on that programme is Angus Fraser. The grumpiest man ever to play cricket, yet one of the loveliest you will ever find. Hardworking, honest, consistent, skilful and grumpy. Those five adjectives best describe a fast bowler who at times produced some real magic in an England shirt and would have done it more if it wasn't for injury. However, his consistency was his greatest trait as a cricketer. As a captain you could rely on Gus. You knew what you were going to get and you could work out a strategy based on what he would give you. He took his wickets cheaply, and he never let a batsman get away with anything they didn't earn. He took those same principles with him into his journalistic career as a thoughtful and honest writer, and he is using them again as the boss at his beloved Middlesex County Cricket Club. Gus is one of the game's great servants.*

ANGUS FRASER – WATCH OUT, FRASER'S ABOUT

Telling stories about playing days in the dressing room can be tricky because there are some things that should remain within the four walls, yet some things are just funny and silly and shine a light on the fun side of the game and the players.

I think the game has changed a fair bit for the better since my playing days. There is more knowledge now about things like nutrition and fitness than there was when I played. That isn't to say we didn't work hard; it was just done differently. We draw on the advances in science and technology to try and make the players and the game better than before, and in large part it works, but we don't always succeed.

You could argue that because the players are full-time and train all year round they are more elite in what they do now; or you could contend that they are less rounded because they don't go and work in the real world during the winter. What I don't think has changed is the mentality of a 20-year-old lad who is getting to play his favourite sport for a living and wants to have fun. It was the same when I was that age and it is the same now – though perhaps some of the pranks have changed slightly.

I'm not sure how I'd react if the following happened in my dressing room now, and if any of my players is reading this then don't even think about it!

As a younger player in a Middlesex dressing room full of established international-class cricketers like John Emburey, Mike Gatting and Phil Edmonds, it was a great environment in which to play the game but also a lot of fun. One day we were trying to save a game up at Nottinghamshire and, not really thinking about the state of the match, I thought it would be funny to stretch a condom over the top of Simon 'Yozzer' Hughes' bat handle. Obviously the condom was covered in lubricant and this made grasping the bat extremely difficult. I figured that he wasn't particularly useful with it at the best of times, so what the heck.

Embers was batting out in the middle and trying to dig us out of a hole when Keith Brown got out and Yozzer went in. He didn't even notice the condom. He got out to the middle and started batting, but obviously couldn't grip it too well. He removed the condom and still struggled because both his gloves and the bat handle were now greasy.

At the other end Embers was playing with a bat he wasn't entirely happy with. It was almost about to break. So when Yozzer got out, clean bowled, Embers demanded that he give him his bat to use. Yozzer didn't put up much resistance and handed it over. I went out to join Embers in the middle and, after a few balls, he came up to me and moaned about the 'oily' bat that Yozzer had, wondering what he did with it. I kept quiet.

Next ball Embers was out. In came Norman Cowans, who didn't last too long, and we lost the game. By the time we got back to the pavilion, Embers knew all about the condom and my part in it and gave me the most frightful bollocking about mucking about during a game. Yozzer thought it was hilarious, but I never tampered with his bat again.

That wasn't the first time a prank had gone wrong for me, though. During one of my very first games in the first team at Lord's I decided to have a bit of fun in the lunch room. Now, Lord's lunches were made famous by a wonderful lady called Nancy Doyle, who would cook up some amazing food for the players and, if you got into her good books, she would treat you very well indeed.

One such player was Wayne 'Diamond' Daniel. Our teara-way Bajan fast bowler on the field was immaculate off it and he loved his food. He liked to be looked after just so and, as one of the most likeable men you could ever meet, it was easy to see why Nancy loved him. He was charming, polite and very appreciative.

So, on this particular day, Nancy had cooked a steak for Diamond, and he was ready to tuck in, when he leaned over for a salt cellar to sprinkle a bit over his food. Whoosh! All the salt fell out on to his steak, thanks to yours truly. Don't ask me why, but at that time I thought it might be funny to loosen the top of the cellar to see what would happen.

Wayne jumped up and cursed, more in genuine upset than anger. 'What's wrong Wayne dear?' asked Nancy as she came rushing out of the kitchen.

'My lovely steak has been ruined by the salt. It all just came out and now look at it.'

Nancy knew exactly what had happened and, as I was the only person in the room with Wayne, she turned to me and shouted, 'What do you think you're doing, you little f**ker! I spend all my time slaving away in that kitchen and you think it's acceptable to behave like this!

'You're a disgrace young man. How would you like it if I made a mess of all your hard work? And what about Wayne, does your team-mate not deserve any lunch? . . .' and on it went for a good five minutes. I've had bollockings from captains, senior players, coaches, punters and chief executives, but in 30 years in cricket no one has given me a dressing-down quite like Nancy did that day. I spent the rest of my Middlesex and England career at Lord's trying to make up for it, and maybe by the time she left in 1996 she'd forgiven me . . . Maybe.

There is no job in sport tougher than being a cricket captain, and I should know after my attempts at it. But when someone comes along who is tailor-made for the role, they can make it look ridiculously easy and the most important thing is that they take their team with them. Think Mike Brearley for England, Viv Richards for the West Indies, Allan Border for Australia and Sourav Ganguly for India. Sourav was the perfect man to lead India at a time when the whole country was emerging as a global force. India was changing and Sourav was the man to embrace the traditions of the old and the boldness of the new. He was a fine batsman who looked at home in a middle order of wonderfully talented players and set India on their way to the Test and World Cup successes they have had in recent years. He was the right leader at the right time.

SOURAV GANGULY – TROUBLES IN ENGLAND

During the 2002 tour of England I had one of the most testing times as India captain. Most people will associate that tour with my exuberant celebrations during the one-day series at Lord's, when I lost myself for a moment or two. However, there was another moment that will stay with me forever.

We were up in Durham for a match at Chester-le-Street and we were being looked after at Lumley Castle, a beautiful hotel that overlooks the ground. As captain I was taken up to my suite and I must say it was a magnificent room with everything you could want. We finished training for the day, with the match

81

due to be played the following morning, and I went back to my room before heading out for dinner. When I returned, I wanted to get an early night and be fresh for the match. I closed the curtains, switched off all the lights and climbed into bed. I cannot sleep with any lights on at all.

I fell into what I thought was a deep sleep, but then was awoken by the running of the taps in the bathroom. I got up, switched on the lights and went to turn off the water. The taps were already off. I thought I must have dreamt it or heard it from another room. I went back to bed, making sure everything was turned off and the place was quiet, then fell back asleep.

Probably half an hour later I was woken again by the sound of running water. I got up quickly and went to turn the taps off. They were already off. This was now really strange. I didn't know what was going on. I decided to get back into bed and keep the lights on, to see if I could sleep that way, but I couldn't – I just lay awake, listening to the silence of Durham.

This was ridiculous because I needed to get some sleep ahead of the match. I got up, turned everything off again, convinced myself that I was being silly and went back to bed. A third time I was woken up by the taps. I jumped out of bed and ran out of the room. I was terrified.

I went to Robin Singh's room, knocked on his door and asked if I could come in and stay in his room. He asked me what was wrong. Now, I was the captain, so I couldn't tell him I was scared and was worried about ghosts, could I? I told him that the heating was broken in my room and it was too hot, so I had to come and sleep on his floor. He said absolutely, but he couldn't have the captain on the floor; I must have his bed and he would sleep on the floor. I told him the floor would be fine and he was very kind to let me stay.

I never stayed at Lumley Castle again, and it made me chuckle when I heard that the West Indians in 2004 and the Australians in 2005 had a similar experience with the Lumley ghost. I'm sure it is friendly, but I didn't want to find out!

On a completely different note, I was once playing at Durham for Lancashire when my parents flew into London from India to visit me. I had totally forgotten to make arrangements to have them picked up or transferred to Manchester, so I thought I had better go and get them myself. I didn't really think it through because it is just about the furthest journey you could do and I was in the middle of a game. Still, I finished the day's play at six, got into my car, drove down to Heathrow, picked them up and arrived back in Durham at three in the morning so that I could play the next day. Needless to say, I didn't have the greatest day.

However, I will almost always drive myself around when I'm in England now, after one of the most terrifying moments of my life travelling on the London Underground. It was back in 1996, on my first tour to England. We were staying in the Cavendish in Piccadilly and things were going just fine. One afternoon we had a bit of time free so I thought I would go and visit some family in Pinner, which is in northwest London. Navjot Singh Sidhu was with me and he said he would come along for the ride.

We got on the tube and set off towards Pinner. In our carriage there was a group of young teenagers, two boys and three girls, and they were drinking. We were sitting opposite them and I could see that one of them was looking at us while he was drinking his beer.

I didn't really get a good feeling about him and I tried to avert my eyes and look at other things. As the train rumbled on I could see that they were getting quite restless, and as this one lad finished his drink he flicked his can straight at us. I could tell he was looking for some kind of reaction. I didn't want to get involved at all and I said to Sidhu to leave it alone. I picked up the can and put it to one side, at which point the young lad stood up and said to me, 'What did you just say?'

I told him I didn't say anything, but Sidhu jumped in and confronted him. I knew then that there was going to be some trouble. I took my glasses off and threw them to the floor away from us, and got ready for whatever was to come. There were some punches thrown and, just as we got to a station, I pushed the lad and he fell over. He got up and the next thing I saw was a gun in my face. I thought, My gosh, this is it – my life is going to be over here on this train. But then one of the girls, who was quite big, grabbed him and pulled him away and took him off the train. She was really quite strong and I don't think the young boy wanted to mess with her. I was shaking and obviously very upset, but thankfully my tour and my life were able to continue.

I became a regular driver in the UK after that, so when I played for Lancashire a car was part of the package. I had a flat near the ground, very close to Old Trafford, the football stadium. At times, though, I was a bit lonely up there because my friends and family in England were down in Pinner. One Thursday I was in my flat, at a loose end because we didn't have a game until the Sunday. I thought I would go and visit my family and then head back up on the Saturday night.

As it happened there was a bit of a gathering on that Satur-day, so I decided I would stay the night and then get up early on the Sunday to drive back up to Manchester. If I left at about 6.30 that morning I would make it easily in time for the warm-up before the 11 o'clock start. I set my alarm clock and went to bed. At 8.30 my uncle came into my room and offered me a cup of tea. I had missed my alarm and was going to miss the game. I got dressed quickly, ran downstairs and set off for Manchester. Now, I probably shouldn't admit to this but I was so worried that Bob Simpson, our coach, was going to drop me that I just put my foot down hard on the accelerator and prayed that I would get there. At about 10 o'clock I got a call asking where I was, and I told them I was in Manchester but there was a little bit of traffic and I would be a few minutes late.

I got a second call at 10.30, again asking where I was and why I was missing the warm- up. Again I said the traffic was terrible, even though I was flying up the motorway and very close to the ground. It was simple, they said – either I got there by 10.45 or I was dropped.

I didn't think I would make it, but I squeezed every last drop out of my Mercedes and at 10.44 on the dot I pulled into the car park. I had got away with it and I was playing. Bob was a smart man, though, and just before we went out onto the field he said to me, 'Those motorways can be terrible at this time, eh Sourav?'

'Yes, coach, terrible,' I replied a little nervously.

'Especially the M1, eh?' he said.

'Yes, especially the M1, coach,' I replied.

He just smiled back at me, and I immediately realised he'd got me. He knew exactly why I was late, and this was his way of letting me know that he knew. He didn't have a go at me or bring it up again, but I understood that this was my warning, and I wasn't late again . . . For a long while at least!

When I think of all the friends I have made playing this wonderful game my brain starts to hurt – and, before you say it, that is not just because I'm using it! It is because there are so many I struggle to remember them all. But one man I will always be in touch with and be firm friends with is Sunil Gavaskar, the original little master. He was a sublime batsman of the highest quality, and along with his incredible technique he had the patience of a saint. He didn't mind how long it took as long as he stayed out there and batted his team into a position of strength. Guys like him and Geoff Boycott are a bowler's best friend because you've always got time to put your feet up when they are batting. The problem is when you're the opposition and you've got to keep running in all day at them. He is a good man off the field, too. We make sure we always find time for a catch-up when our respective teams are playing each other and there is no greater pleasure in this world than following Sunny to Trishna restaurant in Mumbai where you will be served the best food in India.

SUNIL GAVASKAR – BETTER THE JOKE'S NOT ON YOU

Playing for the Indian cricket team can be a stressful job. It can be a difficult place to be when you go out to bat carrying the hopes of so many people with you, especially if things aren't going so well. Fortunately, the Indian team has enjoyed plenty of success over the years and, when you're a part of that, there's nowhere better. Even now, when I see the current generation doing well, I notice the difference it makes to people's lives and the whole mood of the country changes.

In the dressing room, though, you have to try and block it out. You have to try and keep yourself on an even keel and not worry too much about the pressure from outside.

The dressing room can become a haven from what is going on in the real world, and I loved that environment. I had worked for a cement company before becoming a professional cricketer, so I knew what normal people's lives were all about. I never thought my life would be playing the game I loved and looking after my family as a result of it.

As seriously as I took what I did on the field, I also wanted to have a bit of fun, and the dressing room is where I enjoyed myself. Ask any of my team-mates and they will tell you that I used to play a few jokes on them, that was just my way of releasing a bit of tension. When I was younger I used to be a fan of scary masks, the sort you could buy in the joke shop especially around Halloween. On a tour to New Zealand I once found the perfect shop selling lots of different masks, so I popped in and bought a couple. One was a scary-looking mask with a bald head and long white hair around the sides, a bit like Hulk Hogan's hairstyle.

We were staying in a hotel in Auckland and each room had a balcony outside. The balconies were so close together that you could easily climb over from one to another. So after practice one afternoon I decided to put on my mask, wrap myself in a white sheet and climb over the balcony to next door. I could see through a gap in the curtains that one of my team-mates had just come out of the shower and was busy checking himself out in the mirror. He was very happily admiring his muscles with just a towel around his waist, at which point I tapped on the window and gave him the fright of his life. He was so scared that he ran out of his room and into another team-mate's room on the opposite side of the corridor.

He was lucky that all of us used to keep our doors open because as he ran he lost his towel and he was in no mood to stop and pick it up! This naked cricketer had to explain why he'd just burst into another's room, by which time I had climbed back over the balcony, got rid of the mask and the sheet and walked out to find out what had happened. If I could have stopped myself laughing I think I would have got away with it. But it was just too funny, and the boys knew it was me. That player has to remain nameless because he does quite an important job now; but still, he remembers.

Playing the prank is always better than being on the end of it, so I made sure I played my fair share. But back in 1980 when I spent my only season in English county cricket, I was on the end of one from a certain I.T. Botham.

Viv Richards was away playing for the West Indies on their tour to England, so I was asked to step in and play for Somerset and I was only too happy to oblige. Even though England were busy playing throughout the summer, in between the matches Beefy would come back and play for the county, and having got to know him a bit when we'd toured the previous year, we had a good time together. Now, if there was one man who liked playing jokes on people more than me it was Beefy and, after having a chat one day about dogs, he decided to play one on me.

I have never been a fan of dogs ever since I was a small child. It is not that I had a bad experience or anything like that. I just had a bit of a fear of them as a youngster and it stayed with me. I'm not too bad with them now, although Ravi Shastri has two at his home called Bouncer and Beamer and like most batsmen I'm not too fond of them!

In those days there were obviously no mobile phones, so if you wanted to make a call either you had to go and ask permission to use the club office phone round the other side from the dressing rooms, or you just nipped out the back to the red phone box. During a break in play I went to the phone box and made a couple of calls. While I was in the box Beefy came out with his dog, an Alsatian, and proceeded to leave him just outside the door. Now I was trapped. I didn't want to get out with this dog sitting there, and Beefy just left him and walked away.

After a few minutes there were about three or four people waiting to use the phone, and they were shouting at me to get out, but I wouldn't. I told them if they moved the dog then I would leave, but no one wanted to move it because it didn't belong to them. Luckily they were Somerset supporters so they knew who I was, but they didn't go and get Beefy for me either. I had to stay in that phone box for about 20 minutes until Beefy came back, laughing his head off and asking if I wanted anything. By now I was getting a bit angry and told him to move his dog once and for all. He made as if to walk away again, so I pleaded, 'Beefy! Beefy! Please!'

'You only had to say please,' he smiled and finally took his dog away and let me out. I was so relieved. Normally I would swear my revenge on someone for something like that, but I know that Beefy is such a dog lover that he might bring his whole pack next time! I still owe him for that one, though.

I've always enjoyed my time in England, although as a player I once got a ticking-off for doing something that I thought was the right thing. It was the last Test of the series against England in 1974 at Edgbaston, and Bill Alley was standing in his first Test match as an umpire. He had umpired a couple of our tour matches and he was a nice guy and I got on well with him.

We batted first and I took the first ball as usual. It was a short ball that bounced a touch and nipped back in, so as I tried to leave it, it brushed my glove on the way through to the keeper. The players appealed, but they didn't need to as I walked straight off and back to the dressing room. I didn't think there was any problem with it.

At lunch, I was on my way to the dining room when Bill motioned for me to join him in the umpire's room. I didn't know what was going on. He hung up his coat and then laid into me. 'What do you think you were doing, Sunny?!' he said.

'I don't know what you mean,' I replied, more than a little perplexed.

I had always been brought up to play the game the right way. If you hit the bat and are caught then you walk off. I realise this is not something that most players do anymore, but back in the 1970s it was still the norm and I thought I had behaved honourably, even though you could say it was embarrassing to be out first ball of a match.

'I can't believe you did that to me, Sunny! My first Test match, my first over and my first bloody ball in Test cricket and you couldn't even let me get my finger up and make the decision!'

I had no idea just how much decision-making meant to umpires until that moment. They care about getting things right and doing a good job in front of all the people watching as much as we cared about scoring runs and taking wickets. I could only apologise profusely to Bill and, as I left the room, I promised him he could make the next one . . . if I got out, that is.

I have come across plenty of high-quality nicknames in my time in sport, but none beats Ashley Giles' moniker 'King of Spain'. It was all down to a printing error on a set of mugs to commemorate his benefit year – they should, of course, have read 'King of Spin', but the way in which both he and his fans latched on to it and made it his own was tremendous. At first I couldn't understand why there were Spanish flags being unfurled at England cricket matches, until it was pointed out who they were for. I'm not sure many other players would have got the same treatment, but such is the affection for Giles in the game and from the fans that it just worked. Always a competitive cricketer, his attitude and manner meant that he was universally liked and respected as a bloke, and that is huge credit to him. His ability with the ball as a left-arm spinner was hardly earth-shattering, but he was so consistent that he always gave the team something. He always contributed in some way and on the odd occasion he would be a match-winner, and you can't ask for much more. I'm delighted he has stayed in the game as a cricket coach and we can now see him pass on his style, skill and knowledge to players at the highest level, which can only be a good thing.

ASHLEY GILES – THE TOURING LIFE FOR ME

A lot of people who see me coaching the England one-day team containing a few players I once shared a dressing room with will think that it hasn't been that long since I was in there playing, too. In some respects they are right – six years can feel like no time at all. However, it certainly didn't feel that way as I looked at the differences between the touring life I had and the one now open to the current crop.

On the field things are largely the same. Players might be a touch fitter and a touch more professional as the game continues to try and improve; they might also have one or two new shots in their locker as the Twenty20 game has encouraged ever more innovation; but essentially the game I played for England during the early 2000s is still the game being played now.

Where things are a world apart is off the field and the way in which players spend their free time on tour, which I saw for myself on a recent trip to India.

I can remember on my first Test tour to Pakistan in 2000 we actually went up the Khyber Pass when we were in Peshawar. To think about going there now would just be impossible – we don't even go to Pakistan, let alone go on adventures while there. Even back in 2000 we had to have a truckload of army guys in front of us and behind us just as a precaution, but we didn't really feel like we were in danger. It was just a thrilling adventure.

We took the bus right to the edge of Afghanistan and looked over the plains at this barren, jagged and fearsome landscape. It was quite stunning and also a bit foreboding, but we had a great time. There were a couple of gunning areas where I remember having a photo taken with Andy Caddick – I still have that snap somewhere at home. On the way back we stopped at a local leader's house and had a real celebratory afternoon, with a bit of a banquet and dancers performing.

At the time you take those things for granted because you just think that is what happens on an England tour and at some point you'll probably be back, but on reflection I now think what a special memory that is to have.

We also stopped in a couple of bazaars and, ever the typical young sportsmen with time on their hands, we were all looking for dodgy DVDs, but there were shops selling AK-47s, gunbelts and grenades. It was like a scene out of *Rambo* if I'm honest, so we knew we were somewhere a bit different. We were being asked if we wanted to purchase the artillery or at least fire off a few rounds, but sensibly we left the military kit behind and stuck to cricket. It really was an amazing trip and, with everything that followed, I guess we were lucky to be able to go there and see what we did when we did because I don't think any of the current crop of players will get that chance. That is where things are so different.

The more exotic and adventurous trips are not really open to the players much anymore due to security fears and a need to be that bit more cautious. They are effectively kept under a very tight watch for their own safety, especially in parts of the subcontinent, which is a necessity but also a bit of a shame.

There is also less time on tour now than ever before. Schedules are packed so tightly, with so much more cricket played, that there are fewer days off to be able to go and explore like I did when I first started playing international cricket. In 2002 I toured India and was able to go and see the Taj Mahal. I had never been to such a beautiful and tranquil place. Despite there being so many people around, I couldn't get over how quiet and peaceful it was. There was something very special about it, and it was the sort of experience that you have to pinch yourself about.

While the players might not get the chance to go out and about quite as much, they have certainly got the upper hand in the technology department back at the hotel. In my day we relied heavily on DVDs, but now the boys have quite a range of things to play with, from Cooky's dartboard to the Xbox.

I went into Craig Kieswetter's room in Delhi and he had his iPad set up with speakers and music blaring, there was the Xbox, which was set up on a projector against a wall – because obviously a TV is too small these days – and on the floor was a remote-controlled toy helicopter. I did have a chuckle to myself and think, Is this how touring has developed?! We were lucky to have a DVD player that worked and a pack of cards. Communication with home is on a different level, too, with video calls through Skype a far cry from a crackly line that kept cutting out. Whereas the main issue on arrival in a team hotel in my day was a comfortable room and well-stocked bar, the immediate concern is now the bandwidth for the Wi-Fi.

In Pakistan we were all on one floor, with all the doors open, and people would be in and out of each other's rooms, chatting, relaxing and enjoying each other's company. If you were lucky you might be able to smuggle a bottle of something in and have a couple of drinks, talking about the game and life in general. It was a type of team bonding and it was good fun. The players still have that time together, but the banter flows over a game of FIFA rather than a Jack Daniel's.

One activity I'm sure we won't see players practising again is the classic tuk-tuk races we used to have in Sri Lanka along the coastal front of our hotel. The fact that Zimbabwe captain Heath Streak dislocated his shoulder falling out of one told us how dangerous the three-wheelers can be, but before that mishap we enjoyed them to the full.

I think it was physio Dean Conway's idea, with coach Duncan

Fletcher's backing. Players were teamed up in pairs with eight tuk-tuks lined up at the entrance of the hotel. We all had to do a couple of press-ups and then sprint to our machines. Once squeezed in, it was up to the driver to get the most out of the little motor in a race up the beach front, around the grassy central reservation and then back again. Of course, there were a couple of cheats who tried to cut across the grass and were immediately disqualified. Former England skipper Mike Atherton was one of the naughty competitors. There were bribes for the drivers left, right and centre, but the tuk-tuk used by Craig White and yours truly battled it out fair and square. Our only problem was a slight weight distribution issue, in that we had a lot of it, compared to the winning vehicle that contained Graham Thorpe and Mark Butcher. Another Surrey carve-up!

FRED THE ENFORCER

Up until recently there used to be a phrase among those in English cricket who had experienced it called 'being Freddied'.

It, of course, referred to the heroic all-rounder Andrew 'Freddie' Flintoff and how you would feel after a night out with the big man. Following his pro-boxing debut, 'being Freddied' could now mean having your head punched in, which ironically is exactly how you felt after a night out with him. Many have tried to keep pace, but only one or two have succeeded to tell the tale.

Plenty of people have taken their pot shots at Freddie over the years and it all came to a head following his pedalo escapade in St Lucia during the 2007 World Cup. I would argue that none of those who were quick to judge him and have a go has any idea of just how hard he had fought for England over the years and just how hard it was physically for him to do the incredible things he did on a cricket field. This guy put his body through the mill for England. Pounding in the way he did for over after over and then going out and striking the cricket ball as fiercely as he did took some guts and real bravery, something that seemed to be forgotten in the beachside vitriol aimed at him.

There was nothing wrong with Freddie letting off a bit of steam following the Ashes in 2005; in fact, everyone revelled in it. 'Good old Fred' they all said; he puts his body on the line and then has a drink to wind down.

In the aftermath of a 5–0 Ashes defeat and a World Cup that was going horribly wrong, Fred tried to ease the pressure in the same way and was castigated for it. I didn't think that was fair.

Let's be clear, Flintoff was not the only England cricketer using that option throughout that tour, but because he was the highest profile, thanks to his match-winning ability, he was the one taken down furthest. From what I heard it was a pretty good night, though! A few rum and Cokes, some music and great company. Just what an evening in the Caribbean should be like.

It was a particularly difficult time for Fred following the Ashes, but I think it is important for people to realise that life was not always like this for him. You will have seen how hard he worked getting himself into shape for his boxing match with my old mate Barry McGuigan. He has discipline and courage and that is a side that is just as strong as the fun-time Freddie image, and he showed it throughout his career. Still, that didn't stop others getting Freddied.

A case in point was during the New Zealand tour in 2002, which was probably the start of his emergence as a high-quality all-rounder. He had already performed brilliantly in India on his one-day 'not bad for a fat lad' tour and was on a real fitness kick in determination to produce his best for England. The only problem was that during the New Zealand tour one of his good friends, the Press Association cricket correspondent Myles Hodgson, was having his stag do before getting married in the USA.

All the media men were there in Wellington for the evening's festivities and Freddie wanted to be there too, but he couldn't drink because England still had work to do in the series. He could have politely excused himself, but that wasn't Fred's style. As promised, he turned up and had a few glasses of lemonade.

The rest of the pack, though, were free to drink to their heart's content. A few drinking games ensued and, in this situation, you need a fines master, someone to keep an eye on people and make sure they drink when and what they're supposed to. Who better than a sober Fred to take charge. Armed with a bottle of vodka in one hand he took on the role with relish.

Get something wrong and Fred was next to you in a flash, pouring grog down your neck. One or two tried to stop him, but they clearly forgot how strong a six-foot-four burly all-rounder can be. Any resistance was futile; Fred won the battle and a few hours later a decidedly heavy-legged group of journalists took the war to a local night spot called Mermaids.

The selling point of Mermaids, so I'm told, is that it is not like any normal gentleman's club. Yes, there are women dancing around in a state of semi-nakedness, but there are also giant water tanks in which they swim and float alluringly, hence the name. Performing for drunken men from the UK is par for the course, but when one of them sheds his clothes down to his underpants and jumps in with you then that is beyond the call of duty.

The swimming miscreant shall remain nameless, but he knows who he is and let's just say there aren't too many members of the media following the England team on tour who could fit into a mermaid tank, but he found it ever so easy. Unfortunately no one was able to take a good photo of the incident, but apparently it was very cold water indeed.

Graham Gooch was the most dependable English batsman of his generation, and I have never known a man to enjoy batting more than him. A good thing, too, because he faced more balls than any Englishman has ever done before or since. If he wasn't batting for England he was batting for Essex, and if he wasn't batting for them he was in the nets working on his game. He just loved cricket. To see him now at the age he is, still working with England cricketers, passing on his vast knowledge and giving them the throw-downs they need, is a testament to how much he cares about the game and English cricket. He is a man for whom I've always had a tremendous amount of respect and his contribution to the game has been remarkable. We will never see another Goochie.

GRAHAM GOOCH – WHAT A WAY TO GET OUT

When you've finished your career and you reflect on the memorable days you've had, naturally you remember the days you were at your best and the hundreds which you scored. I was lucky enough to score a few for England and Essex and they were all special to me – as I tell the players these days it is not about how, it's how many!

Scoring a hundred is the benchmark for a batsman, but it is not the end point; it is only the first of what could be two or three hundreds. These are the big scores that make a difference to your team and it is the sort of detail that people remember. Yet, when I talk to people about my career one of the things I get asked about more than any other is not my 333 at Lord's or any of the other hundreds – they want to know about when I got out because I handled the ball.

It was such a rare way of getting out that it has taken on a life of its own, and people don't even recall the circumstances surrounding it. As far as I'm concerned it wasn't so much about an 'odd' way of getting out, it was a dismissal that stopped me from saving a game against the Australians which could have had a huge effect on Ashes cricket over the next few years.

I had been totally focused on trying to dig England out of a hole and had made it to my century during a decent partnership with Graeme Hick. If we could stick together out there, then we had a chance of denying Australia. Merv Hughes had been pounding in for over after over and I felt like I was playing him pretty well when I defended one and it somehow managed to bounce under my bat and was heading towards the stumps. Instinctively I just knocked it away with my hand and I thought I might get away with it, but my old Essex team-mate, Mark Waugh, was fielding in the slips and he said: 'Oi, you can't do that, mate – that's out.'

Of course he was right, but Dickie Bird was the umpire and he wasn't sure what to do. He really didn't want to give me out in a controversial way, but he had no choice. To this day I don't know why I did it. If I'd used my bat there wouldn't have been a problem. Since it happened, a few others have gone the same way, perhaps most memorably Michael Vaughan against India, but what few people realise is that it wasn't the first game that I'd played in where someone had got out for handling the ball. Back in 1992 we were on tour in New Zealand and played against an Emerging New Zealand XI. In their side was a useful all-rounder called Justin Vaughan, who went on to become the chief executive of New Zealand cricket. He had batted for over an hour and survived pretty well, even against my medium pacers, but then when Phil Tufnell managed to sneak one through his defences the ball trickled back towards the stumps and, for some inexplicable reason, Justin bent down and swept the ball away from the stumps with his glove. No one could quite believe it when it would actually have been easier to use the bat. Just like me it was instinctive and when it dawned on him what he'd done, he could hardly bring himself to walk off the pitch.

It is a feeling every cricketer has experienced at some point in their career, where they can't quite accept how they've managed to get out and take an age to get off. Some players take out their frustration in the dressing room, with a throw of the bat or a few expletives, others sit quietly and don't say a word or perhaps seek solace in the shower. My old mate 'JK' Lever took the strangest approach to getting out I had ever seen, and this was in only my third ever first-class match.

It was early on in the 1974 season and Essex were playing Sussex down at Hove. It was a particularly interesting three-day game and we needed a getable 219 to win on the final day. Before the redevelopment, the changing rooms were over to one side of the ground and above them was a viewing deck where the opposition could go and watch the game. I was sitting up there with JK and he was being bullish about our chances. In particular he didn't have much time for their overseas off spinner, a chap called Uday Joshi. It wasn't anything personal but JK just didn't rate him. He was going on and on about how could this bloke get anyone out, he didn't spin it and he was easy to pick up and send over the ropes, all the usual bravado.

In any case Joshi had picked up three wickets and was bowling just fine. For some reason I was batting down at eight and went into bat with 97 still required. I put on a decent partnership with Stuart Turner, so that by the time I'm the eighth wicket down we need just six to win. I get back on the viewing platform and JK is still banging on about Joshi, to the point where he said: 'That bloke will never get me out. If I have to bat and he gets me out, I am not coming back to the dressing room.'

At that moment the ninth wicket falls and we still need four runs to win. Ray East gets a couple off John Snow and then JK hits a single, so with one to win he is facing Joshi. The game is as good as won. The ball is bowled, JK goes back to cut and he gets an edge straight to Alan Mansell at slip and the game is tied. A terrific match finishes, but as all the players shake hands and walk off towards the pavilion, there is one who refuses to join them. Instead, he walks off in completely the opposite direction, clambers over the picket fence surrounding the boundary and, with his pads on, climbs into one of those old deckchairs that they have and sits down, arms crossed, not talking to anyone. JK stays there, motionless, for a good half an hour until finally the anger and shame subside and he trudges back to the dressing room, by which time most players are already in the bar.

It was in the bar that Uday Joshi comes up to me and asks what was wrong with JK. Now, I couldn't tell him the truth, could I? 'He really wanted to win that game,' I offer. 'It just means so much to him.'

Beefy's Cricket Tales

Joshi nods his head: 'That is something I've always found with English cricketers, they care so deeply about the game. Pass on my thanks for a terrific match.'

Now he knows.

David Gower is the finest English batsman I ever played with. There were plenty of others who were in the top bracket, but 'Lubo' as we call him (after an Aussie steakhouse) was a cut above. He was and is also a mischievous bugger with a great sense of fun. We played almost all of our international cricket together, touring the world, meeting new people and seeing new things, and thank goodness David was just as adventurous as me. Perhaps not as thirsty, but we had some great times all over the world, and the best times of all were usually following an England win. There is no doubt that Lubo is an England cricketing great, but also simply a great man to have in your dressing room.

DAVID GOWER – WATCH WHAT YOU EAT

Being paid to play cricket is a wonderful thing. I was lucky enough to do it for many years and the fun I had in the process was what made it so special. Most of the fun to be had usually came on the field of play, and usually against Australia, but that wasn't exclusively the case. There was plenty to be had off the field and in the skies of Australia, too.

Sharing a dressing room throughout the years with the likes of Ian Botham and Bob Willis, not to mention Allan Lamb and Robin Smith, meant smiles and laughter were never too far behind. Since retiring from the game I've managed to go from one dressing room to another in the Sky Sports commentary box, and despite the difference in eras among us the banter and the jokes are just as rife.

Beefy is often at the heart of it, whether it is putting Nasser Hussain's shoes in the freezer or cutting holes in Michael Atherton's socks, but I believe the funniest episode of all actually befell Mr Botham himself on a tour of South Africa a couple of years back. He has long enjoyed being the centre of attention and with a November birthday it means he often gets to celebrate it on tour.

During this particular trip to South Africa a few of us decamped to Leopard Hills game reserve, which Beefy and I have been visiting for many a year and where the staff and the owners have become very good friends of ours. Over the years Beefy has enjoyed the wildlife, the hospitality and, of course, the fantastic South African wines on offer. For those who haven't been caught up in one of Beefy's sessions it can be a chastening experience – and several of the staff at Leopard Hills can vouch for that!

With it being Beefy's birthday a special party was planned for that evening. As usual we went out for our early morning drive. We saw some remarkable creatures and enjoyed a wonderful few hours. We returned for a spot of lunch and a few glasses of vino before getting ready for our second outing of the day. It wasn't too long a drive because we had to get back for the evening's festivities.

As the sun set over the plains we were all tucking into our barbecue and a little more of the wine, and a good time was being had by all. If you can picture the scene: we were sitting in one of those large African tents with just the fading sun and the dim candlelight to guide our eyes, and with our glasses constantly filled it was a happy and relaxed evening among friends, at which point the music started. Since Beefy is such an old friend of the place they had arranged for some dancers and musicians from the local village to come up and put on a bit of a show to wish him happy birthday. He loved it.

The drums then fell silent and out came the birthday cake. A few more candles were lit and happy birthday was sung; a round of applause and a big grin from Beefy.

'Now, Mr Botham, you must cut the cake,' said one of the staff.

He cut it and lay down the knife.

'Now, Mr Botham, you must taste the cake,' said the same man.

It was a beautifully iced, round chocolate cake, exactly the kind Beefy likes. He opened wide and took a huge bite out of this gorgeous confection. Just one chew was enough and he spat it out, lurching back in his chair, eyes wide like a big cat chasing her prey.

'What the . . . !!' yelled Beefy, before gulping the wine faster than he has ever done before.

The entire room was in fits of laughter, including the American guests, who really had no idea who anyone was but still found it all rather amusing.

'Why, Mr Botham, do you not like elephant dung?' came the innocent question from the staff member, who could not hide his pleasure at just how well their practical joke had turned out.

Beefy took it well, I must admit. He got his own back for sure over the course of the next few days, as drinks were poured and punishments suffered by anyone who had even dared laugh at his misfortune. But we all agreed thereafter that it had been worth it.

'Whispering Death' has got to be the best nickname ever and it defined Michael Holding to a tee. The smooth, almost silent, run-up to the wicket, the sort of run-up that suggested he could have been equally successful as a 400 metre runner. That was the whispering part. Once he got to the crease and let go of the ball, one of two things usually happened: either he almost killed you with the pace and venom of the ball – and many still have the bruises to prove it – or he knocked over your stumps and you heard the 'death rattle'. Either one of those was the death part. He had pace, control and aggression as a fast bowler and that is why he took so many wickets. Off the field, he is one of the best men I have the honour of calling my friend. He is a supreme gentleman with forthright views on anything to do with cricket and plenty more besides, and he is great company. I'm just glad I get to spend as much time as I do with him now that we are both commentators. Life is far less dangerous sitting next to him than it was with him 22 yards away.

MICHAEL HOLDING – FROM FOE TO FRIEND

In the period of time when I was playing cricket for Jamaica and the West Indies, the game became very serious for us round about 1975 after our tour to Australia and we decided enough was enough. We weren't going to be the whipping boys anymore and under Clive Lloyd we were going to take things very seriously indeed. It didn't mean we didn't enjoy ourselves, because winning Test matches and series all round the world was a lot of fun and there was a lot of laughter in our dressing room, but none of it was silly. There weren't too many practical jokes played in those days, just the usual quick-witted banter that comes from men who talk fast and think even faster.

Back in 1973 Jamaica were playing against the Combined Islands in St Vincent and we had just finished bowling them out. It wasn't too long before the end of play but our batsmen still had to go out and face a few overs. Maurice Foster was the captain of Jamaica and the openers as usual were padded up and ready to go out.

Scheduled to bat at No. 3 was Lawrence Rowe, who was the undoubted star of West Indian cricket at that time. He had announced himself with a double hundred and hundred on his Test debut and was dominating bowlers wherever he played. He was the best batsman around and was our star man for both Jamaica and the West Indies.

We also had a fella called Leonard Levy, an off spinner who came in at No. 11 for us, but he knew how to hold a bat. He might not score many runs but he could defend his wicket.

Anyway, just as the openers went out to bat, Maurice Foster turned to Leonard and said, 'Uncle Sonny [that was his nickname], pad up!'

Sonny Levy had just come off the field having bowled a fair few overs, and was sitting down looking weary and feeling a bit flat. He turned to Maurice Foster and said, 'Skipper, what, me?'

'Yes, yes, I want you to pad up as nightwatchman. It is getting a bit murky out there, we're getting to the end of the day and I don't want Lawrence Rowe to be going out there if we lose a wicket. I'm not sure he will be able to see it that well.'

To which Uncle Sonny replied: 'But skip, if the world's best batsman can't see it then how on earth am I going to see it!'

Well, Maurice Foster couldn't argue with that logic and as the rest of the dressing room broke down in laughter, even Lawrence Rowe admitted he probably had a better chance of seeing the day out than Uncle Sonny. After much grumbling and moaning, Uncle Sonny put his pads on and, sure enough, a wicket fell and he had to go out and face a few balls to get us to the close.

He defended his wicket stoutly and made sure he was still there at the close. On his return to the dressing room, Lawrence Rowe produced a drink for the nightwatchman. Uncle Sonny turned to Lawrence, thanked him and said to the rest of us, 'It is always nice to have a drink from the second best batsman in the world.'

As I said, things tended to be pretty serious in the West Indies dressing room in the 1970s and 1980s, none more so than in 1976 on tour to England, when Tony Greig gave his now infamous interview about making us grovel. Not everyone saw it, but enough of us did to ensure that at our first team meeting after the interview it was mentioned in full chapter and verse. It was something that had a huge binding effect on our dressing room, and I can't remember too many times when everyone was so united against a particular player.

It meant that each time Tony came to the crease every fast bowler found an extra yard of pace because they were so fired up. The problem for Tony and England was that our new era had just started by the time of that tour and we were in no mood to let a provocation like that go. Word got back to us that not only was Tony under pressure for saying it in the first place, but his team-mates didn't particularly enjoy batting with him because they knew when he got to the middle the whole intensity of the game would go up a notch. We preyed on that, too.

What people might not know is that during that series Tony Greig wanted to try to sign me for Sussex in the County Championship. Well, he arranged the meeting through Clive Lloyd and put it to me. That must have been one of the shortest meetings he's ever had because in the back of my mind I knew I wasn't going to play for Tony after what he'd said. The same feelings surfaced again when Lloydy called me from Trinidad to ask me about playing World Series Cricket and said: 'Two people will come and see you in Jamaica.'

'Okay. Who are they?'

'Tony Greig and Austin Robertson.'

Even in 1977 I didn't want to hear from the man, see him or talk to him. I carried the feeling of anger towards him from that one comment for quite some time because I didn't know him personally.

Eventually I went along with World Series Cricket because of Clive Lloyd and my respect for him, and it was only after that tournament that I started to get to know Tony.

Following that series we became great friends and I really appreciated the part he played in changing the game and the lot of cricketers for the better. I discovered on that trip just how much he loved Blue Mountain coffee from Jamaica, so from then on whenever I went to Australia I always took him some as a little gift.

When you are playing cricket, dressing rooms can be very awkward places at times, but the game binds you all together and, even out of anger, some great friendships can flourish and I'm glad to say that Tony and I had one of them. It was a friendship that was able to grow due to our work together as commentators, so when we lost him over the 2013 New Year I was as devastated as anyone at his passing. All I know is that I'm glad we were able to share the time we did, even when I was bowling at him.

As one half of a long line of cricketing brothers to play for England, Adam Hollioake is an example of a true warrior cricketer who never knows when he is beaten. He played the game as tough as they come, yet off the field he was a fun-loving, laid-back guy who enjoyed life to the full. He was perhaps never quite as laid-back as his brother, Ben, or as naturally talented, but he made up for it with his competitive instincts. He was a big reason why Surrey had as much trophy-winning success as they did during the late 1990s and early 2000s under his captaincy. It is one thing to have the talented players he had at his disposal; it is another to get the best out of them, and that is why England gave him the one-day captaincy for a spell. It didn't quite work in the same way for England, but he gave it everything and earned a lot of respect, certainly from me.

ADAM HOLLIOAKE – SPAR A THOUGHT

Before I tell this story, I want to make one thing absolutely clear: I love Alex Tudor like a brother. He is a tremendous fella who is much loved and respected throughout the cricket world, and by none more so than me. He knows this, and when you read the following tale you have to take it in the spirit in which it all happened, which is two team-mates and friends doing what team-mates and friends do – only it didn't quite go according to plan, and there is no bragging whatsoever involved.

Those who know what I'm up to now as a professional boxer and mixed martial arts fighter will realise that I have always had an interest and a respect for fighters and athletes who fight. I get the biggest adrenaline rush of my life when I step into a ring – it takes a lot of hard work, sacrifice and dedication from both men to be in a position to go hammer and tongs at each other. I've always loved that aspect of sport and the bravery it takes to front up to your opposite combatant and take him on. Even in a non-contact sport like cricket I loved that sort of contest, when a fast bowler was steaming in at you as a batsman and it was a case of hit or be hit.

Anyway, while I was at Surrey, I used to train in the winter using boxing and sparring as one of my fitness tools. One year I thought I would take my little brother Ben and his mate Alex along with me, because I thought as two young lads on the staff it would be good for them. They hadn't done it much, but they were really talented sportsmen and both had good hands and feet. Still, it wasn't really fair for me to go toe-to-toe with them when I'd been doing it for a fair few years.

The rules we came up with were as follows: they could hit me wherever they wanted, but I wouldn't be allowed to hit them above the shoulder. It worked and the two of them enjoyed the sessions and I think they got a lot out of it. The only problem from my point of view was that, by not being able to land any shots to the head, every time I led with a punch that had to be lowered, Tudes would come round the other side and catch me on the head. It was fine, but after a while he started to grow in confidence. When he became quite handy at picking off a shot to the head, the banter would start.

'I schooled you, Smokes!' he would say after a session, and I would smile and remind him that if it had been a proper fight he wouldn't be so cocky.

We'd been training like this for about two years when there was a rain delay during one match and not much happening, so we went down into the gym for a bit. I was sparring with some-one else and Tudes said: 'Come on man, let's do a bit.'

'Okay, but if we do it I'm not just taking the body – I can hit you wherever, just like you can hit me.'

We both agreed to this and got the gloves on and started mess-ing about. It was all going fine, but each time he jabbed me he was bringing his hands back a little bit low, and I told him, 'Keep your hands up, they're too low and I can come over the top.'

I told him four or five times, and then he jabbed and caught me with quite a sharp blow and instinctively I just hit him. It wasn't the hardest punch in the world, but it just caught him flush on the side of his face and he went down like a 20-storey block of flats being demolished. The legs went and the body followed – he was gone. I tried to catch him to stop him from hitting the hard floor, but he's a big boy and I couldn't hold him. He was out for the count, but he soon came round and was just a bit dazed.

There were two problems, though. Firstly, a few of the boys, including Alec Stewart, had watched the whole thing, so there was no getting away from what had happened and Tudes was going to be in for a bit of ribbing for going down, and me for laying out a team-mate. The other hitch was that five minutes later the umpires came in and said the rain had stopped and we'd going back out soon . . . and we were bowling! All I could think was, Holy shit, I've knocked out our strike fast bowler and we need him to bowl!

He was in no shape to bowl that day and had to sit things out for a while. He came back and bowled later on with a thumping headache, which showed his bravery and his toughness.

What I would say is that, after that, he got a bit of banter from the lads, who can be pretty harsh at times, and I didn't like it when they called him 'Glass Jaw Tudor' and such like because none of them were brave enough to step into a ring with me. I genuinely didn't mean to do it. The worst thing a fighter can be seen as is a bit of a bully and that isn't me. Now I'm a professional fighter I never spar too hard with fighters who are inexperienced, and I always make sure I look after my training partners.

Others found that episode a lot funnier than I did for obvious reasons, but a couple of years later there was an incident at The Oval which had me crying with laughter. It was just after the quarter-final of the first ever Twenty20 competition and Mark Ramprakash had inevitably been scoring millions of runs. Every time he picked up a bat and walked out to the middle he came back with a hundred to his name. As a result, he was picking up every award going, whether it was player of the month in the championship, player of the month in the one-day competition, man of the match, or just the 'I've got a lot of runs' award – you name it, he got it.

So we had finished this game at The Oval and there were all sorts of gongs being dished out. Ramps' name gets called and he goes up for his award. He picks up the giant cheque and stands there waiting for the photo to be taken of him accepting it, but everyone has gone silent and nothing is really happening. We're all trying to work out what is going on, and the Tannoy is blaring out something but it is all a bit distorted and no one can really make out what is being said.

Ramps remains where he is, waiting for the photo, but all the while someone to the side is trying to point out to him that he's not there to pick up the award – he's been called out to present it to a little kid who is standing next to him. The problem is that, by now, the whole thing has gone on a bit too long, so they've got to move on and they start to shoo the little kid away and pretend that the award *is* for Ramps and not the 12-year-old, but he's having none of it. So you've got this stand-off between Ramps and this lad for an award that should have been a special moment, but instead becomes a battle of wills. In the end they are both ushered away from the stage a little perplexed while the rest of the Surrey team are rolling around the outfield in howls of laughter. It was one of the funniest things I've ever seen on a cricket ground.

LIKE FATHER LIKE SON

They say what goes around comes around and it wasn't until I was long retired from cricket that I truly understood the meaning of the phrase. As a young lad trying to make my way as a professional cricketer I wasn't too concerned with the responsibilities of life. The honest truth is that I was only thinking about the wickets I could take and the runs I could score. I suppose I was a bit immature.

It certainly seemed that way when I met a certain I.V.A. Richards, or 'Smokey' as I call him. Viv and I first met when we played for the Somerset under-25s together and he was this bright new talent from the Caribbean who was going to score more runs than anyone else. I was picked as a bowling all-rounder knowing that a bag of wickets would see me move closer to first-team selection.

We played Glamorgan under-25s down at Bath and Viv opened the batting. He scored nought. I managed to hit 91 and get us up to a decent score. When it came to bowling, Viv took five for 25 and won us the game with the ball. I immediately took to him and said, 'You and me will work well together. You take the wickets and I'll score the runs.'

From that point on we were firm friends and we started sharing a flat together in Taunton. I say a flat, but it was more like a condemned building with us teetering above a printer's. There was no electricity, no running water and we had to use candles as both light and heat. It was pretty grim, but at least Viv made his mark in it by writing his bowling figures from that Glamorgan game up on the wall.

When Viv proved his worth with the bat and was given a decent contract, a couple of years later he bought a flat for himself which I thought was incredibly generous. I don't think he invited me to move in with him, but the moment he opened the door to his new place I followed him in one step behind and never left!

Viv was as good as gold and a bit more mature than I was. He would look after himself pretty well in terms of what he ate and how much he drank; I was pretty much the opposite and contributed much more liquid to the fridge than food. We were young, though, and we only wanted to get on with our cricket. We had a similar outlook on life and that brought us close together, and it was a bond that never broke.

Even though I wasn't the most helpful flatmate you could wish to have, living with me in Taunton did come with a perk or two – namely, the ability to jump in the car with a shedload of washing and drive round to my parents' house once a week to visit the Kingdom of Mum. She was incredible to us and I could never thank her enough for what she used to do. We would pop round every a week without fail, and I think after a while Mum used to hate the sight of our clapped-out old banger coming down the street because she knew what it meant.

We would spend the day with her and get fed and watered and have all our washing done, before heading home only to return seven days or so later to do it all again. As a kid I know I took it for granted, but my mum wouldn't have had it any other way. Soon after I had made it into the Somerset team and was on the verge of England honours I married Kath and she took on much of that support for me, which allowed me to keep concentrating on my cricket and doing what I knew best.

Again, I know I took all the work she did behind the scenes for granted, but there is no doubt just how amazing both my mum and Kath were during my playing days. They kept me going and saved me from having to worry about the simple things. It was only after I retired and my son Liam had decided to give cricket a go that I got to see the other side of the coin.

Twenty years after I shared my grotty little flat with Viv, ferrying our clothes back and forth to my mum's, Liam had moved in with Dimi Mascarenhas, as the pair of them played for Hampshire together. Their flat was disgusting. Everything was dirty, whether it was clothes, dishes or the floor. I couldn't believe that young men could live like this, conveniently forgetting my own starting point.

Together Kath and I cleaned his place, washed his clothes and took the pair of them out for lunch until they could eat no more. Then it was off to the supermarket for a full fridgeload of shopping. It was what we had to do as parents and that is when it hit me how life was repeating itself.

Somehow every time we visited, the boys' flat was always in need of something, especially cleaning. Finally, on about the fifth time we went to see them, Kath was again in full cleaning mode and I said enough was enough. I told Liam that he needed to get his act together and take some responsibility. Always quick with a reply, he reminded me of how his grandmother used to look after Viv and me when we were just starting out.

Thinking I'd win the argument as well as give him a little inspiration I told him that, by that stage, I was playing in the

Somerset team and was at least performing on the pitch. If he turned in match-winning performances then the next time we came back we would be happy to help clean and wash for him, but until then he was on his own.

I should have kept my mouth shut. That was in July 1996 while he was still playing second-team cricket. In August 1996 he made his first-class debut against Middlesex and took five for 67!

121

When scientists say they are going to see if there is life out there in the solar system, I can already give them the answer. Yes. I know this because some of the people I have met in more than 40 years in cricket have clearly been operating on another planet and live in their own world, only to pop down to earth to say hello every now and again. One such cricketing whizz is Simon 'Yozzer' Hughes, a very capable and decent county cricketer who has gone on to make his slightly different take on the world a huge advantage in his broadcasting and journalistic career. Yozzer has always done things a little differently and been his own man, and for that I admire him. He was my team-mate at Durham for a year and we had a great time together, and now I see him around the England team doing his media work, where he has carved out a terrific persona as 'the analyst'. It is precisely because he looks at things his own way, picking up on things that others might not see, that makes him ideal for the role.

SIMON HUGHES – HOT TUB ACTION

Playing county cricket for a living is brilliant. It doesn't matter whether you get to do it for one summer or for 20, it remains the finest way to earn an income, and for all the ups and downs, the vast majority of your time is spent smiling, laughing and joking with team-mates and others.

There is a whole raft of characters in a cricket dressing room and during my time as a Middlesex player I think I got to see the full spectrum that the game has to offer. Yet none of them comes close to the strangest of the lot: Harold 'Dickie' Bird.

Dickie Bird was *the* umpire of his generation and a couple more besides. He was very competent at his job, a bit of a not-outer, but crucially he got on with the players, and if you have a rapport with an umpire you are much more likely to forgive the odd decision you feel hard done by.

We were down in Southampton for a NatWest Trophy knock-out game against Hampshire and Dickie Bird was the umpire. On this particular day the rain was getting in the way of the action. Weather interruptions were Dickie's favourites because it gave him something to fret about, especially during a Test match when all eyes and all cameras were on him. At a lowly county match there was less room for a performance, so Dickie would spend much of his time milling around the dressing rooms look-ing for people to chat and tell stories to. Of course, we'd heard many of them several times over but that never stopped him.

On the day in question, the weather made sure there would be no play until the afternoon so we simply had to put our feet up and wait. Dickie came into our dressing room for a chat, but there wasn't too much enthusiasm from the Middlesex team. He hovered around for a while and was beginning to get on the nerves of one or two players, so I said: 'Come on, Dickie, let's go to the gym. Bring your kit.'

At Southampton there was a gym, a sauna and a Jacuzzi. We went into the gym for a little bit, did a few bits and bobs, and then I told him we'd go for a Jacuzzi. Unbeknown to me, Dickie had never heard of a Jacuzzi, much less used one. Still, he got in and sat there for a bit as the bubbles got going and did what they were supposed to. We got out, by which time the weather had cleared up a bit and it looked like we would soon be able to start.

Hampshire had won the toss and decided to bat, and at the top of their order for the shortened game was Robin Smith. I was opening the bowling for Middlesex and had to be right on the money. I came trundling in from Dickie's end and bowled the first ball, which was cut with customary power and near enough took Mark Ramprakash's hands off fielding at cover point. Thankfully, a four was saved.

The next ball I came in and pitched it up, only to watch Robin crunch it with even more power through the covers where Desmond Haynes took the full force on his body, but crucially another boundary was saved. Robin clearly had his eye in and was looking to take me apart, so it is fair to say that I was a little bit nervous coming in to bowl my third ball. I steeled myself for it, set off a little quicker and focused on what I wanted to do when the umpire stuck out his left arm and stopped me in my tracks. There must have been something wrong with the batsman, I thought, or even an issue with the pitch, or maybe more rain was on the way.

Dickie held his arm out and as I got to him he turned, looked at me and said: 'EEEeee, Simon, it were grand in that bubble bath weren't it?' I didn't know what to say. He had stopped the game just to pass comment on his first ever Jacuzzi. In these modern times, perhaps we forget just how special our first Jacuzzi is.

Nasser Hussain was one of England's most competitive batsmen and one our greatest captains. He is slightly less grumpy now than when he was skipper, but his angry attitude was exactly what England needed when he came along and they were officially the worst cricket team in the world. It was simply unacceptable in his eyes and he moved heaven and earth to get them back on track and for that we should be grateful. I don't think I'm going too far when I say that neither Michael Vaughan nor Andrew Strauss would have enjoyed anywhere near the success they had if it wasn't for Nasser's achievements during his time as captain. Enough of the praise. He is still a pain in the neck in the commentary box and he's the tightest man I know.

NASSER HUSSAIN – WORKING WITH COACHES

If you played for England in the 1990s then you would have come into contact with two of the biggest characters in the game. Ray Illingworth was one, who was a master tactician as a player, but perhaps slightly less so as a manager. The other was David 'Bumble' Lloyd, who cared deeply and passionately about England almost to the point of fanaticism. He is also mad. Not in the wild-eyed, aggressive sort of way, but in the eccentric English sort of way. He had a skewed view of the world and the game, and it would soon bubble to the surface at the first sign of any stress or strain – and, to be perfectly honest, there wasn't a lot else in and around the England team in those days.

Still, we all loved Bumble and playing for him was rarely dull, but he took it all so personally. If we won he was on top of the world, but if we lost then things were about to cave in. There was no middle ground.

One of the more bizarre episodes was on a tour to New Zealand in 1997 when Bumble was coach and Mike Atherton was captain. We had won the toss on a green top in Auckland and decided to bowl. The ball should have done all sorts and our seamers should have been licking their lips at the thought of using a new ball in these conditions. However, from the moment Dominic Cork let the first ball go, things were not quite right. New Zealand's openers could hardly reach the ball it was so wide, and Alan Mullally wasn't doing much better. He was firing one down leg, the other way outside off and, although the scoreboard wasn't exactly motoring, by lunch there wasn't anything in the wickets column either.

Atherton was going ballistic and as Darren Gough walked off he complained about the shape of the pitch. For those who don't know, Eden Park is a rugby ground; they drop in the cricket pitch and have it pointing diagonally across the ground to make for better and bigger boundaries. It does look strange at first, but a five-year-old could grasp the concept in a minute or two. Not Goughie.

Atherton was not best pleased, but at least thought our coach could have a word or two with the bowlers and get us back on track, but when we reached the dressing room he was nowhere to be seen. We thought he had nipped to the dining room for some lunch but he wasn't there either. At that moment some-one looked out the window and on to the second ground behind the stands, and there was our coach pacing around muttering to himself, in obvious distress at how we had bowled in the first session.

'Bumble's officially lost it,' said Alec Stewart over lunch, at which point our coach finally came up to join us and prove Stewie right.

He gave us both barrels for what had been pretty poor bowling, but just as he started to calm down, he asked why it had been so bad. Goughie said, 'I can't bowl on this pitch because the wicket is in the wrong position pointing to fine leg. I'm confused and I've lost my bearings.'

Well, that was it for Bumble. He stormed back out of the dressing room, picked up a chair, strode out to the middle of the second pitch again and sat with his back to the main ground in a huff.

It wasn't to be the last time that Bumble's emotions got the better of him. Two winters later we were in Hobart just before Christmas, in between the third and fourth Ashes Tests. It had been a miserable tour with lots of injuries, but worst of all we were 2–0 down with just two Tests left to play.

The game at Hobart was against an Australia A team that was as strong as a full Test side. Both myself and Stewie had been given the game off so Ath stepped into the familiar role as captain and, on a flat belter, rather enjoyed himself, hitting a double hundred. The match should have meandered to a straightforward draw, but for some reason Ath thought that wasn't good for the game and declared, setting the Australians a highly improbable 376 to win. The bowlers were not happy at all at being made to get back out in the field and run in again.

Cue Greg Blewett's demolition job, hitting 213 not out from 180 balls as the home team won by nine wickets. The tension in the dressing room was more than a little uncomfortable at the end of play. For some reason that only Goughie can explain, he found a Santa's suit from somewhere and came in with little jokey presents for everyone. 'Here's a pillow for Ath, to help him sleep after booking himself in for bed and breakfast on that pitch, and here's a first aid kit for Gus Fraser, so he can tend to those bowling figures and patch them up a bit.'

At which point Fraser lost the plot and went for Goughie. The whole dressing room erupted and it was all kicking off, with Bumble somewhere in the middle trying to calm things down.

The next day we flew to Melbourne to prepare for the Boxing Day Test. When we landed word got round that Bumble had resigned after the earlier defeats and the Hobart debacle. A few of the senior players went to speak to him, but we couldn't find him anywhere. We searched Melbourne airport high and low, before we finally discovered him bending the ear of the lady at the duty free perfume counter. He was telling her why he had quit and the look on her face when we came to take him away was one of quiet relief.

There we were in Melbourne airport, arms around our coach, urging him not to resign, but to stick it out because we needed him and he was a good coach. He needed that show of affection, I think, because he changed his mind, stayed on and we only went and won in Melbourne. It was to be the last live Ashes win until 2005 and Bumble celebrated that victory as if what had gone before had never happened.

He loves his cricket perhaps more than any man I know and, just like his personality in the commentary box, he loves it to be fun. Some of us have perhaps taken it all too seriously at times, but people like Bumble are needed just as much as the serious types because ultimately playing cricket should be fun, no matter the level.

At times with England, Bumble's successor as coach, Duncan Fletcher, and I were accused of not being enough fun, and while I agree we took our jobs very seriously, it is not true to suggest we never let the players enjoy themselves. In fact, I can remember one incident where Freddie Flintoff enjoyed himself so much it left me in agony for a good few days.

Duncan arrived in the England job from Glamorgan, where he had been coach of a very successful side, and he brought with him some of the antics from the Welsh dressing room, one of which was to be big on team fines. This would be a little bit of a mickey-taking exercise: players would either have to drink certain amounts depending on what they'd done wrong, or if we didn't have a day off the next day then you would be made to do something embarrassing or feel a little pain. In charge of the fines was Dean Conway, the physio, and in charge of the punishments was Freddie Flintoff, because he could enforce them as the biggest and strongest member of the side. We all took to calling him 'Mungo', after a giant cartoon character.

In South Africa in 1999, we were having a fines session and I had been pinged for something ridiculous, like failing to shut a door or something similar, and Fred made his way over. This time the punishment was just to have Fred sit on you for a period of time and if you argued then you got a bit of a slap. Freddie had had a couple of drinks and was relishing his role, so when I kicked up a bit of a fuss he made sure he gave me a good slap – only he really doesn't know his own strength and he left a hand print on my back for about a week!

It was agony and poor old Duncan thought I was so upset that I was actually going to leave Freddie out of the side for it. I teased Duncan about that, but Freddie carried on playing and I made sure I was beyond reproach for the remaining fines meetings.

If variety is the spice of life then every team needs a Mark Ilott, both for his left-arm-over seam bowling – a precious rarity – and his dressing-room banter. He wasn't given the nickname 'Ramble' for nothing. Guys like Ramble are the lifeblood of a dressing room. They can pick people up when they're down, they can keep the energy of a team high just by cracking jokes and getting everyone laughing, and when they've got the ability on the pitch to back it up as well then they really are a captain's gem. Sadly, injury denied Ramble the chance to play more than the five Test matches he did, because clearly his county form for Essex showed he had the ability to be a top bowler if only his body would back him up. He was the perfect replacement for Neil Foster and he should have enjoyed a similar international career but Essex rather than England got the best of him.

MARK ILOTT – GOING TOE-TO-TOE

Playing in the Essex side of the early 1990s was to be among some of the very best cricketers in the land, and as I was breaking through I learnt an awful lot about the game from guys who had been there and done it all. It was a lively dressing room with plenty of big characters, such as Derek Pringle, Don Topley, Neil Foster and Graham Gooch, who had all brought home plenty of silverware down the years.

But as always there was a natural refreshing of a great team and the younger faces were all keen to make their mark on the field. One lad who wasn't too shy in coming forward was Nasser Hussain, who went on to become one of the greatest captains England has ever had, and his fiery nature never left him throughout his career. He's mellowed a touch now, but when he was younger he could be particularly feisty.

Now, Nas was my best mate in the team and we're still good pals, but there was one particular incident which shows that even the best of friends have their moments in dressing-room life. We were playing against Kent at Tunbridge Wells in 1992 and I was fielding down at fine leg after a lengthy bowl during that morning's session. Bowling the over before lunch was our overseas player, Mark Waugh.

As every bowler knows, when it's the final over of the session you want to make sure the batsman has to play at every ball because he's under a little bit of pressure not wanting to get out before the break. Mark certainly knew this and, as a superb all-round cricketer and a very capable swing bowler, he would have expected to get it right. On this occasion he wasn't quite on target and, bowling to Carl Hooper, he slipped the first ball down the leg side.

Nasser was fielding in the slips and piped up with something like, 'Come on, Tugga, get your line right. He's right-handed, you know.'

There is so much nonsense talked on a cricket field that most of it washes over you, especially as a bowler. I often wondered why people shouted things that were so bleeding obvious that they served no real purpose at all, yet they still get said all the time. Telling a bowler to 'get your line right' was like telling a batsman 'don't get out to this one!' But you learn to live with it and it's all part of the game's background noise.

Mark came in to bowl the next ball and this too slipped down the leg side.

'Come on, Tugga, he's still right-handed,' said Nas.

The third time the ball went down the leg side, Nas came out with another comment only for Mark to stop and turn to him, saying: 'Is there any chance you could just stand at slip and shut the f**k up and let me get on with doing with what I'm doing?'

Nasser was a talented cricketer and a big part of the side, but he was still one of the younger guys and our stand-in captain, Neil Foster, thought he should know his place.

As I mentioned, I was down at fine leg thinking about my baked potato for lunch, so when the over was finally finished, I motioned to the batsmen to say well played and effectively ask if I could walk off ahead of them since I was practically in the dressing room already. They nodded and off I went. Having bowled a fair bit and worked up a sweat, I wanted to have a quick shower and freshen up. Unbeknown to me, as the players leave the field, Neil Foster has given Nasser an earful for his comments to Mark and basically told him to keep quiet. This hasn't gone down very well with Nas, who is absolutely ticking by the time he makes it to the dressing room.

By now, I'm stark naked, just as nature intended, and about to go into the shower. Nasser thunders into the room and lashes out at the first thing he sees, which happens to be Nadeem Shahid's 'coffin'. Now, it wasn't the biggest changing room at Tunbridge Wells so as he's kicked the hard-sided bag it has slid across the floor and rammed straight into my right big toe. It was absolute agony and I let out an almighty scream as the rest of the team were filing through the door.

The reason for this was not because I was a big girl's blouse – no matter what anyone else says – but because as a fast bowler the big toe on the landing foot, which was the right in my case, is always in a state of disrepair. It gets a pounding and a half as you ram it into the front of the boot, putting several times your bodyweight through it. There is a lot of pressure and that's why you often saw holes cut out of the top of boots to help relieve it. Getting a newspaper land on that toe would have been painful, so a coffin was something else, and after five or six seconds I still hadn't heard a word from Nasser's lips. All it needed was 'sorry, mate' or 'didn't mean to catch you there, Ramble', but there was nothing. So I turned round and said sarcastically, 'Oh, don't worry about me, mate,' which meant, 'Where's my apology, you idiot?'

Instead of taking the hint Nasser turned and said, 'Have you got a problem with that?', to which I replied, 'Well, yeah, actually I have', at which point he lunged at me like a flying squirrel and grabbed me by the throat. That sounds quite dramatic, but considering the state of undress I was in, if he'd grabbed me by anything else I really would have been in trouble.

He pinned me up against the wall and demanded, 'What are you going to do about it?' The red mist had descended and I wasn't really interested in having a naked wrestle with Nasser when he was in that mood. Thankfully, Paul Prichard sprang into action and split the two of us up before it got any worse.

I went and had my shower and thought that would be the end of the matter because these things happen and they stay in the changing room. However, word got back to Graham Gooch, who had been away with England, and he called me up wanting to know what had occurred. I didn't want to tell him because I knew it would get Nasser in trouble, but Goochie said he already knew the details; he just needed to hear it from me. I confirmed what he knew and, consequently, Nasser was banned for the next two games as punishment and had to go and play in the seconds. He wasn't happy at all with that, especially as one of the games he missed was against new boys Durham, who most batsmen fancied playing at that time.

His first game back was at Headingley and, travelling independently, he arrived before us. He was out in the middle checking the pitch when I ventured towards him, not sure what his reaction would be – this was supposed to be my great mate, after all.

As I got closer I could see he was smiling, so I gave him a bear hug and he apologised. He said that if it had been anyone else he probably wouldn't have reacted that way, but because we were mates he thought he could get away with it.

It wasn't the last time Nasser would fall out with someone – in fact, he probably managed it in that very next game – but we remain firm friends to this day.

Anyone who bats and bowls and takes catches for his team is all right in my book, and for Essex and England Ronnie Irani fits right into that category. A top bloke with a great sense of humour, Ronnie is the perfect man to have in the dressing room. He always gave his team everything he had but he wanted to have fun doing it. He loved the game so much, and he played it the right way. He always has something funny to say no matter what the situation, so the fact he presented a breakfast radio show was perfect for him because he could try out all those gags on people needing a little pick-me-up in the mornings.

RONNIE IRANI – STRETCHING THE AUSSIES

Back in 2003, I had joined up with the England one-day side in Australia for the games that followed the Ashes. England had been getting an absolute caning in the Test series, as was usually the way before 2005, and spirits were clearly a little low on the trip, as you might imagine. They were 3–0 down after three Tests and the one-day series had come along as a bit of respite. They were starting the VB Series, between us, Australia and Sri Lanka, midway through the Test series for some reason, with the Boxing Day and New Year's Tests still to come.

With the one-dayers there were one or two newer faces, who added a bit of life to things – there was myself, Freddie Flintoff, who was getting back to full fitness, and young Jimmy Anderson, who had just come up from the academy. We're at Sydney for the first of these one-day matches and we're getting another proper pummelling from the Aussies.

I'd bowled my first spell and done okay, but Australia's batsmen were in the form of their lives and just cracking on with it. Adam Gilchrist and Matthew Hayden at the top of the order just blasted our bowling all over the SCG and there was very little we could do.

We had got 250 in our 50 overs thanks to Nick Knight's 111 not out and, although it wasn't a massive score, in those pre-Twenty20 days you felt you were right in the game with that sort of total.

The Aussies made it look very small the way they went after us and by the time I finished my spell the game was clearly only going one way. As the match was drawing to a close it looked like the slow bowlers would have the winning runs hit off them. As luck would have it, there were still a few runs needed, so Nasser shouted down to me, 'Ronnie, you need to get ready, you'll be on in a bit.'

I thought, Cheers, Nas! The Aussies are smashing it into next week, the game is over and you want me to warm up again. It's clear you've never warmed up in your life after a spell.

What came out was: 'For f**k's sake, Nas!'

'I know, pal, I'm sorry,' he replied. 'Someone's got to bowl the overs and it might as well be you!'

I retreat down to fine leg, and I'm stiff as a board and wondering what I've done for my old Essex pal Nasser to pick me for this. My body's not happy in the cool, damp Sydney evening air. It was warm during the day, but this is a day/nighter and I've seized up and really need to be on a rack to get me stretched out again. Anyway, I start my stretches and warming up with my arms, and I hear this cheer go up behind me. To begin with I think nothing of it because it's late in the game and I reckon a few drinks have been sunk. They're probably making one of those beer snakes with their empty plastic glasses.

So there I am, stretching my hamstrings and quads, and then I start moving from side to side to stretch out what bowlers call the grunt muscles – the sides of your torso which take a bit of a workout when you bowl. Just as I start moving from side to side the cheers get a bit louder and more regular, and I'm now thinking, Oh Christ, they're doing it at me! And any cricketer will tell you that, whatever you do, don't take the crowd on, especially an Australian crowd because they will batter you.

There is no love lost between an Aussie crowd baying for a Pom-beating and a lone bowler down at fine leg. There has been some unbelievable abuse over the years for English bowlers in Oz and I wasn't keen to get them started. After about my third or fourth stretch it became clear they were having some fun, so I turned round – and saw 10,000 people side-stretching along with me.

My immediate thought was that Nasser was going to get the right hump with this because he could be a grumpy sod even at the best of times. His team were taking a battering in the Ashes, getting smashed in this one-day game, and here I am stretching for the fun of thousands of Aussies . . . Nasser is not going to be happy about this. But I didn't care. Sometimes we forget that cricket and sport are about having fun so I decided, Bo**ocks to it, if Nasser can't see the funny side to this then he is even more of a miserable so-and-so than I thought.

I turned round and carried on stretching and the crowd were loving it. They all went with me and we were having some great banter. Someone even threw down this fancy-dress pumpkin hat, so I put it on and we had a right good laugh. At the end of it all the crowd went wild and clearly loved it. And finally, two months into the tour, we got the first smile from Nasser! If you type 'funny English cricket player' into YouTube, you will see what I'm talking about.

It was a light-hearted moment in a difficult tour and, as it happened, we actually played some decent cricket in that one-day series and got to the final, where Australia beat us before going on to win the World Cup later that year. It was just the right time for a bit of fun and, to be honest, if the game wasn't already dead and buried I don't think I would have done it or got as involved in it as I did.

The funny thing was that the Aussies really took to me after that. They used to do something similar with Merv Hughes years ago and I think they adopted me as a replacement, someone to have a bit of fun with. I couldn't believe how crazy it was for the next few days, though, as the clip got played on all the TV stations in Australia as well as back home. I became a bit of a higher profile player thanks to my stretching exercises, which was ridiculous.

We went on to Canberra a few days later and I can remember going out for dinner with my old Essex team-mate, Mark Waugh. Now, this guy is a legend of the game, and certainly an icon in Australia when it comes to cricket. We'd just pulled up at the restaurant and were getting out of the taxi when this bloke comes up to me and says, 'Hey, mate, you're that Ronnie Irani, aren't you? The England cricketer?'

'Yes, I am.'

'Oh, mate, you're a champion, you're a legend! It's great to see you, mate, you're a champion. Can I have your autograph?'

I'm standing there next to Mark bloody Waugh and this guy's asking for *my* autograph first. I sign his piece of paper and then I push it over for Mark to sign and the bloke says to him, 'Oi, you're not having that – it's mine!'

At which point I had to put him straight about who it was and why he should sign it. He tried to make out he knew who it was all along but he didn't fool Mark, who signed the piece of paper 'Best Wishes, Steve Waugh'.

When it comes to being a professional cricketer, you'd have had to search far and wide to find a more professional player than Steve James. As a determined opening batsman for a decade and a half for Glamorgan, 'Sid' wrung every last drop of effort and energy out of his body and made himself one of Wales's own. A disciplined trainer and fitness fanatic, he was also a smart cricketer and it is no surprise to see him carving out a successful career as a journalist now that his playing days are over. He knows plenty about the game, but perhaps rugby is his greatest love because his writing on the oval ball game is as incisive and passionate as any former player doing the same.

STEVE JAMES – FINE DINING

Playing for Glamorgan during the 1990s was an experience to treasure. We had a group of players who were not only very good at what they did, like Hugh Morris, Matthew Maynard, Steve Watkin and Adrian Dale, but they were also terrific blokes who made for a lively and often funny dressing room. Through that period we also had a few bona fide legends of the game in there too, such as Viv Richards, Waqar Younis and Jacques Kallis, who all added to our squad on and off the field. It meant we had successes to go with our fun, which made them all the sweeter, such as the Sunday League title in 1993 and the County Championship in 1997.

During some of that time we had former Zimbabwean cricketer Duncan Fletcher as our coach and we got on pretty well. He obviously went on to bigger and better things with England and then India, but I think he really enjoyed his time with us and he was a real laugh back then, too.

With our Southern African connections we would go to Zimbabwe for our pre-season tour and on one of those trips, after playing a hard day's cricket in the searing heat, we all needed a bit of feeding and watering. That is an area the Zimbabweans certainly knew how to take care of. You trained hard and you played hard, so once we had all showered off and changed there was a terrific hog roast and bucket of cold beers for us to get stuck into. We didn't need inviting twice.

It was the perfect setting. We were gathered around the pavilion, tucking into our food and drink, and there was lots of merriment and laughter. That all reached a crescendo when Darren Thomas piped up after finishing his plate: "Ere, mate, grab us another bit of beef from that pig will you!'

Now, I should point out that Darren was not the sharpest tool in the box and this sort of comment was par for the course from our pace-bowling all-rounder. But one evening in 1997 he truly outdid himself.

Whenever we played away Duncan thought it was important that we all had one meal together as a squad. It was a good idea because it meant that we spent a little bit of time with each other away from the cricket field and, while they were not always raucous events, they were usually a good laugh. Each time it was up to a different player to choose and book the restaurant, and we had some interesting choices. Essentially, though, the checklist was for a place that did decent food – not too cheap, not too pricey – and was somewhere we could all feel comfortable.

We were playing Lancashire up in Liverpool and Duncan turned to Darren and said: 'Right, then, it's your turn to book the restaurant. Don't muck it up – just choose something sensible.'

'No problem, coach,' said Darren. 'You can rely on me.'

Later that day Darren went to speak to the receptionist at our hotel to get some advice on where he should take the lads. As you can imagine, Darren has a broad Welsh accent and, of course, the girl on the desk had a thick Scouse accent, so between them they could look after the BBC's regional voices quota with ease.

'All right, miss, can you help me, please? I'm looking for a classy restaurant to book for the boys, not too pricey mind, but somewhere we can all fit in easily.'

'Not a problem, I've got just the right place for yous lot. It's about ten minutes in a taxi from here and it's called Maisez Vous. Shall I book a table for yous?' she replied.

'Oh, yes, please, that sounds perfect.'

He left rubbing his hands, thinking he'd done well with a nice French restaurant nearby, something that would impress the coach and the players.

Come the evening, we all piled into three cabs and Darren gave the details to each of the drivers before we set off in convoy. I was in the second car and our driver told me he had never heard of it but thought it must be a new restaurant that had popped up. As we followed the cab in front it soon became clear that he was getting a little confused because we'd driven around the same few roads two or three times. This was back in the days before smart phones and immediate internet access so we had to rely on our wits.

The third time we went round the block, two of the cars drew level so the drivers could have a chat about this new restaurant, Maisez Vous. By now we'd been driving for about half an hour and people were growing restless. I could see Darren getting a little worried, too.

It was at that point that I suggested we should go and ask someone in the local pub to see if they knew. We turned the corner and I spotted a Harvester sign. 'Let's stop there and ask.' As we pulled up, I saw the full name of the pub – The Mersey View!

That was the year we won the County Championship and we beat Somerset at Taunton to do it. Having bowled them out for the second time on the third day we were left needing 11 to win the title. Now, myself and Hugh Morris had enjoyed a cracking year as opening partners for Glamorgan, but with just 11 runs needed you're facing an awkward dilemma; you're on a bit of a hiding to nothing, where you think, Someone always gets out chasing such a small total – and you don't really want to be that man. But in this instance, there's also the chance that you'll hit the championship-winning runs, which is huge. I jokingly said in the dressing room I didn't want to go out there, and Matthew Maynard jumped in without a moment's pause and said, 'Don't worry, I'll go out there and do it.' To which I told him to sit down and take his pads off because Hugh and I would be walking out as usual.

I'd had a good year with the bat, but the runs had dried up a bit at the back end of the season and down at Taunton I was up against Andy Caddick, who used to give me heaps of abuse and I back at him. We just never got on, and he had cleaned me up for eight in the first innings. Add into the mix the Whyte and

Mackay rankings, which give individual ratings based on performances. I was top of the batting rankings and he was top of the bowling.

With only 11 needed to win, you might come up against a bowler who will just put it in the slot and not embarrass you, a bit like Jack Nicklaus not making Tony Jacklin putt a little teaser in the Ryder Cup which he could have missed. But with the history between me and Caddick there was no chance of that. He came steaming in and bowled faster than I've ever seen him bowl in my life. Because it was the last game and the rankings were involved he absolutely legged it in and nearly took my head off first ball. Second ball, I'm absolutely plumb LBW but George Sharp, the umpire, says not out.

Two balls later, I nick one and it carries beautifully to Peter Bowler at first slip, a complete dolly catch, and he drops it. The next over, Hugh Morris gets a single and I'm facing Graham Rose. Caddick, who was at fine leg for Hugh, is supposed to move round to be at fine leg for me, but he doesn't. So, when I flick the ball for what I think is a single, the next thing I know is that half of Wales have not only made it down to Taunton, but are swarming on to the pitch because I've just hit the winning boundary.

Beforehand, Adrian Dale, who bats three, had said to me, 'If you're out there, grab me a stump', so I take two stumps with me just as I get engulfed by all these fans.

The crowd hoist me on to their shoulders and start carrying me off. We go about 10 yards and then one of the blokes hits the turf and I come tumbling down with him. As I'm on the ground, my bat and one of the stumps are grabbed out of my hands. So instead of feeling great as I get to the edge of the pavilion, I'm actually really pissed off because I've not only lost my bat but I'm thinking Adrian is going to be upset, too, because the one stump I do have isn't going to him.

At that point I look up and see Adrian – with two stumps in his hands! Hugh has given him one and his brother Gary, who is a policeman, has seen the bloke who nicked it off me and wrestled it off him and given to Adrian. He didn't get my bat back, though.

In the end I made an appeal through the local newspaper, the *South Wales Echo*, and luckily it was returned to me, which restored my faith in the Welsh public.

Anyone with a Test double hundred to their name has to be a more than capable batsman. Robert Key easily fits into that category and, after years of sterling service to Kent as an opening batsman and a captain, I find it bewildering that he doesn't have more than just the one big innings against the Windies. In his 15 Test matches there was enough to suggest that Key could have forged a hugely successful career; his misfortune was to overlap with Marcus Trescothick, Andrew Strauss and Alastair Cook. He took the game to the opposition, which I liked, and he reminded me of my old hero Ken Barrington, who used to impose himself on the game with his presence. Always quick with a smile and a joke, Rob is also extremely thoughtful on the game and I have always been impressed by what he has to say when I've seen him summarise for Sky Sports.

ROBERT KEY – FINDING MURALI

As an international cricketer you get to enjoy all that the highest level of the game has to offer, whether it is touring the world, playing alongside the best in the country or testing yourself against and getting to know the very best in the world. I was fortunate enough to do that for a few years, and of all the players I've met and got to know, there is one who has made me laugh and scratch my head more than any other – Muttiah Muralitharan.

An absolute icon of the game and just a brilliant man, Murali turned my world upside down for half a season in 2003 when he came to join Kent as one of our overseas players and produced some of the best cricket I've ever seen, as well as behaviour that just left me in stitches. Murali is a fantastic human being and there isn't an ounce of malice in him, which is why a lot of the things he does are accompanied with the biggest grin in the game and you can't help but love him.

He is Sri Lanka's greatest export when it comes to cricket and, although he played most of his county cricket up at Lancashire, it was great for us to be able to have him for that summer, and he made a huge impact. In the time he was with us, he took us from bottom of the championship to second that year and he is talked about just as much now as he was back then.

The thing about Murali is that he just doesn't shut up. He might not have a perfect command of the English language but that doesn't stop him, and when he gets a bee in his bonnet he just doesn't let it go. Even though the Kent dressing room has had its fair share of well-heeled and cut-glass accents in its day there has always been a healthy dose of reality there, too. And on entering the sanctity of that room, Murali was presented with an array of choice words that he simply couldn't understand.

The one that most concerned him was the stereotypical name sports teams give to their Welsh or Kiwi colleagues. We had a New Zealand physio called Ian Erickson, who was called 'Sheep-shagger' – not entirely original but the old ones are the best. Murali was fascinated by it and wouldn't stop asking him about it, which made us all laugh because Ian struggled to get across the concept of 13 sheep to every man, woman and child, which is the ratio back in his homeland.

Murali struggled to say the word 'shagger', too, so if ever there was a problem while he was bowling he would just shout 'Sheep!

Sheep!' to get him to come on. After play, if 'Sheep' was busy, he would get his own personal assistant/driver/physio/cook/bag man to look after him. Murali looked after this chap really well, like he did everyone, but he once told me that if Murali was struggling to get to sleep he would come and get him up and ask him to rub his feet for him – even if it was three in the morning!

One day we were playing a championship game against Nottinghamshire up at Trent Bridge and Murali turned up with his man, ready for action. The club had given him his kit the week before and he had two white shirts for the four-day stuff and then two coloured shirts for the one-day games. As he pulled on his silver shirt to go out and field, a few of us thought he was having a joke. He wasn't. He'd put the one-day and champion-ship shirts into the wash together on a high temperature and managed to create a third kit for special occasions. It was 10 minutes before the start of play, so we had to run round to the Notts club shop and buy him a new shirt in which to play. We found a plain white one that didn't have the Notts crest on it and then taped up the sponsor's name on the other side. Still, to all intents and purposes Murali was playing against Notts in one of their own shirts. Did it bother him? Not a chance of it as he took six for 36 to win us the game, and he even signed and presented the shirt to a young lad after the match.

What happened after that game was a brilliant example of Murali's generosity. Not only could he be generous with his money – he was always sneaking off to pay for restaurant bills without telling anyone – but the same was true of his time. He came off after bowling that spell and then sat down with Michael Carberry, who was just coming through, and he spent over an hour just talking to him about batting, passing on the knowledge he'd gathered over the years. He loves cricket so much that he will gladly talk all day about it and pass on what he knows, and he has a lot of knowledge to share.

However, he is also one of the dopiest cricketers I have ever seen. There was a game for Sri Lanka where he was once run out because he left the crease to give Kumar Sangakkara a hug. In a game against Leicestershire, where we were fighting to avoid the follow-on, he went into bat with Martin Saggers and struck a couple of sixes that took us to within 10 runs of getting there. The next over Martin cuts one to point, and they set off, but it is well fielded and Martin shouts, 'No! Get back!' The throw comes in and misses the stumps. Murali is a third of the way down and just stands there, watching the square leg pick it up and underarm it to the bowler. He turns and watches the bowler take the bails off and, throughout, he has not moved from the spot and ends up run out. That is how dozy he could be, but you couldn't be upset with him about things like that. He came back into the dressing room and put together a sentence that contained broken Sinhalese, broken English and a smattering of swear words that would have made Jim Davidson proud. We were learning about the mastery of batting and spin bowling from him and he was developing a mouth like a sewer – it was a fair trade.

However, my overriding memory of a player who really injected a spark into county life for me and all those who played with him took place off the field late one evening. We also had Andrew Symonds in our side that year and, together with Murali, the three of us went out one night to a club in Canterbury. There was me and Symo drinking pints and Murali sipping on his Bacardi Breezer. It didn't take too much to get

Murali excited and that night we had a few, and let me tell you that he cannot, under any circumstances, dance to save his life. We were in the corner of the bar and Murali went off to the toilet. After a little while, Symo wondered where he'd got to. A little more time passed and still no sign, so I went off to look for him. He wasn't in the toilet so I thought someone must have recognised him and was pestering him for a photo or an autograph. Still no sign of him. And then I noticed a bit of a commotion on the dance floor. It was like one of those flash-mob dances where everyone is doing the same moves, only they hadn't arranged it beforehand.

At the centre of this Bollywood-style, Bhangra 'light bulb' dance was a certain Murali, bringing a touch of the subcontinent to Canterbury. His impact was wider than any of us thought it would be.

If Nick Knight had been Australian he would have been a World Cup winner for sure. As one of too few genuine world-class one-day cricketers England produced in the 1990s he was regularly fighting a lone battle to try and pick his side up and join the best in the world. Post-1992 England were left behind in the one-day game as the likes of Sanath Jayasuriya and Adam Gilchrist pointed the way forward, and Nick did everything he could to try and help England keep pace. He was busy, innovative and a fantastic striker of a cricket ball at the top of the order, and with a good enough technique to earn several Test caps, too. His position as a one-day master is beyond doubt, which is why he brings plenty of knowledge and insight to bear in his current role as a commentator. One of the nicest blokes you are ever likely to meet in the game – but don't ask him to change your flat tyre. Practical duties are not his forte!

NICK KNIGHT – TAKING THE MIC

For those who know me in and around the game I've never been one of cricket's great characters like a Darren Gough or a Freddie Flintoff. While they were larger-than-life players, who put in big performances on and off the field and were always the life and soul, I was a little more reserved and only occasionally had my team-mates in fits of giggles. I enjoyed myself as a player, made the most of my ability and was honoured to have played for England in both forms of the game for as much as I did. But even for the quieter members of the dressing room there is always a chance to play a practical joke and make the rest of the team laugh.

After more than a decade as a professional cricketer, and more than five years after my England debut, I took my chance to crack that joke and then sat back as it went horribly, horribly wrong. It was on the 2002/03 Ashes tour that it happened. England were beginning to find some consistency under captain Nasser Hussain and coach Duncan Fletcher, two men I admire hugely and I was grateful to play under. However, the course of my relationship with Fletch didn't always run as smoothly as it might have.

As a coach he has one of the most technically gifted minds in the game and he couldn't fail to improve you as a cricketer in one shape or another. He was also a stickler for time-keeping that bordered on the obsessive. When it came to team meetings, there would be the time the session was due to start, say 2 p.m., and then there was 'Fletcher time', which was 1.45 p.m. I didn't have a problem with it, since I almost always got to where I needed to be in plenty of time . . . except once.

We were in Australia and were due to play in a one-day warm-up match at Bowral Oval. We had already played half the one-day games, but the Boxing Day and New Year's Tests were sandwiched in between the rest, so we had this game against a Bradman XI to help us get our eye in.

Now, the bus was due to leave at 9 a.m. from the hotel, so I was there nice and early and got my seat. Moments before we were due to set off someone from the hotel came on board and said there were two room keys missing and they needed to be handed in before we left. I realised one of them belonged to me, so I jumped down the steps and went to hand mine in. It took a bit longer than it should have done, but imagine my surprise when I went back outside and the bus wasn't there. Fletch had told the driver to go without me.

Just then I spotted Mark Waugh, who was captaining the Bradman XI that day and was an old mate from our time together at Essex. He saw what had happened and asked if I wanted to join him for a cup of tea and then he would give me a lift to the ground. I was relieved not to have to find my own way there.

When we arrived England were already busy warming up for the game and Fletch pretty much ignored me. I opened with Owais Shah, who scored a ton, but we lost the match thanks to an even better hundred from Mark for them.

The next day we flew to Hobart for a VB Series game against Australia. I was sitting next to Nasser and heard the air hostess offer to let him sit in the cockpit with the captain for a while. He wasn't interested but I thought it would be fun so I asked if I could go instead. After being shown the controls and the amazing view that the pilots have, the captain turned on his microphone and started talking to the plane. 'Hello, this is your captain here, we are shortly due to land in Hobart, Tasmania, where the weather is a chilly twenty-four degrees [hot summer for us]. We are delighted to have the England cricket team on board with us today and we hope you have an enjoyable time here, but lose to the Aussies obviously.' With everyone chuckling in their seats I motioned to the captain to pass me the mic and he handed it over.

'In addition, it has come to our attention that one or two of you have had a few timekeeping issues on this trip,' I said with my tongue pressed firmly in my cheek. 'You know who you are and you have been very naughty boys! Don't let it happen again.'

All the lads knew it was a joke and were having a good laugh, and as I made my way back to my seat I felt great, having added to the fun of the trip. Only there was one man on the tour who wasn't laughing. I didn't notice.

That evening I got a call in my room from someone claiming to be Duncan Fletcher. It was clearly our regular prankster and team physio Dean Conway, a barrel-chested Welsh wonder who makes life fun, full stop.

'Nick, your behaviour on that flight was not on,' he said.

'Yeah, yeah, Deano, good one.' And I put the phone down. It rang again seconds later. 'Did you just put the phone down on me? I'm not happy at all, Nick,' he said.

'Whatever, Deano. I'm going to bed now.' And with that I put the phone down again and thought nothing more of it.

The following morning at breakfast I found out exactly who had made the call as Duncan gave me a stare that looked ready to end my career. I was stunned that my one gag had gone down so badly and the coach was now fed up with me. In the end Nasser had to act as peace-maker between the two of us because Fletch had felt so strongly about the whole incident, which was only supposed to be a bit of fun. I was lucky that I was nearing the end of my time as an England player; I retired from international cricket a couple of months later, following the 2003 World Cup. Had I been a young lad I'm not sure I would have got the chance to go out on my terms.

Allan Lamb was one of the bravest cricketers ever to play the game and his continued success against the most fearsome bowling attack in the world, the West Indies, was a testament to that. Every time he played against them he seemed to score a hundred, and it was great to watch. Of course, there was a lot more to Lamby's career than that, including being my partner in off-field antics for much of it. I couldn't have wished for a better team-mate than Lamby; he was always good fun to be around, and we have remained firm friends to this day. For a few years we roomed together on tour, which had its pros and its cons. On the one hand I had a roommate who enjoyed the odd night out and didn't mind if I came back late; but on the other I had a roommate who knew how to turn a phone bill into the length of a phone number and then insisted we halve it!

ALLAN LAMB – NORTHAMPTON'S FINEST

Playing cricket with Beefy for all those years was like a test of stamina in itself. Being in a dressing room with him was a challenge, but for the most part a lot of fun. I think when we were playing, the game on the field was very serious and competitive, but off the field there was a bit more freedom to have fun and enjoy yourself. The game has moved on a lot and become much more professional, although I'm pretty sure there are still a few jokers around who make dressing rooms the special places they have always been.

As a captain I thought guys like Beefy were good for team morale because they would often get people's minds off the pressures of the game. You can sometimes overthink things as a player, but if you've got Beefy putting your shoes in the freezer, or doing stuff like that, your mind isn't on how you got out!

Beefy was a shocker. When he was bored he could be the worst practical joker in the England team. If he'd had an early night then he'd get to the ground and he'd be restless and looking for something to entertain him. He would do silly things like tie a knot in someone's trousers so they couldn't get into them. You'd leave your trousers hanging up on the peg the night before, and then when you came to put them on to go out into the field you couldn't get your legs in them. Sometimes there'd be two or three guys fiddling around with their trousers while the captain was walking out to the middle. People thought we were disorganised, coming out in dribs and drabs, but the truth is that Beefy's knots were a bugger to undo!

At times, when batsmen weren't playing well, he would go round and make a red mark on their bats with a message: 'Please aim here'. He had a short attention span and was like a big kid in the dressing room, which was fun to be around most of the time, but sometimes you just wanted him to settle down. If he'd been out for a big session the night before that was a good thing for the rest of us because he'd be quiet and subdued, so we could count on getting a bit of peace. If he came in and was too frisky, we knew it would be a tough day.

Back at Northamptonshire we had a few wags in the dressing room, and more often than not the butt of their jokes was a guy called David Steele. We used to call him 'Stainless' on account of him never buying a drink. He was one of those blokes who could take a joke and, because of his demeanour, it would somehow be funnier when it happened to him. He used to go round pinching cigarettes. When a few of us got wise to him we'd say we didn't have any, so he would turn to Richard 'Chippy' Williams: 'Ah, Chippy, you've always got some. Give us a cigarette!' And, begrudgingly, Chippy would hand one over.

After a while he'd had enough of this, so Chippy went to a joke shop and bought a packet of these crackers that looked like cigarettes and replaced every single one in his packet.

Stainless and I were batting together at the end of the day and as soon as we came off at the close he went looking for a cigarette. A few of the other players knew what Chippy had done so they made their way out of the dressing room, but were peering in through the window.

Stainless declared: 'My man Chippy will have one!' And went rummaging in his pockets.

He found what he was looking for, took one out of the packet and as he lit it, the cigarette blew up in his face. It gave him the shock of his life, but he didn't stop there. 'There must be something wrong with the lighter. Can you pass me the matches, Lamby?'

I couldn't believe it. Well, I wasn't going to stand in the way of a man and his cigarette. He took another one out of the packet, lit it with the match and boom! It happened again, and poor old Stainless jumped even higher because the last thing he expected was a repeat.

Chippy came back into the dressing room, fully anticipating that Stainless would go mad at him, but all he did was turn to him and say, 'Chippy, you've got a dud pack of cigarettes there, my friend, just to let you know.' Chippy simply smiled and got away with it.

Stainless was just a funny character and blind as a bat, too. When he went into the shower, he would put a pair of thick-rimmed glasses to one side and the only thing for us to do was take them and stick them in the freezer. He didn't like that much, and he could get quite angry. For some reason, though, that didn't stop us; it only made us do it to him more to get a reaction out of him.

One strange habit of his involved a pair of white boxer shorts that he wore regardless. He never changed them and we would moan at him about how smelly and old they were. But he would always pull them on first and then put his jockstrap over them and go out to bat. It was an old joke but one day the boys had just had enough of his white boxers and took a large helping of Deep Heat to them just before he came in to get ready for bat. He put them on and, by the time he'd padded up, he knew something was wrong. But, full credit to him, he didn't take them off. He insisted they were his lucky boxers and he was going to wear them come hell or high water. I batted with him that day and he was on fire. I never saw him move that fast between the wickets ever again.

He was a tough old pro and took whatever was thrown at him on or off the field, and clearly most people will remember him as the 'Bank Clerk Who Went to War' for taking on the Aussies in 1975 and the Windies in 1976. With his white hair and glasses, when he got to the wicket on debut Rod Marsh turned to Dennis Lillee and said, 'Dennis, it looks like your father's come out here to have a bat!

'Hey, grandad. what are you doing out here – did you get lost on the way to the toilet or something?'

He just turned to Marsh and said, 'You see this arse of mine? You're going to be looking at it for a long time, you better get used to it.' And he was right.

BETTER THAN AMBROSE
AND WALSH

Confidence is a must for a professional sportsman. You've got to have faith in what you can do and believe that your best day will be better than that of your opponents. But there is a difference between having confidence in your ability to play the game well and believing you can do the impossible, and if you talk as if you can, you'd better be able to back it up, otherwise you deserve the abuse that comes your way. And in some cases the sledging from off the field can be just as withering as that on it.

There is a funny story about one such player who thought he could do incredible things with a cricket ball, and sometimes he did. His name is Andy Caddick. On a tour of the West Indies in 1998 rain delayed the start of a Test match until late one evening and, with England batting, they had about 20 overs to play before the close. Alec Stewart and Michael Atherton were given a torrid time as per usual by Curtly Ambrose and Courtney Walsh. They were nipping the ball back into them on a regular basis and kept pinning them on the pads and in the ribs. After 13 overs of resistance Ambrose got Atherton LBW with one that nipped back. At the close of play England were 36 for two and were lucky not to have lost more.

The next morning Stewart and the nightwatchman Dean Headley went back out there and, expecting more of the same, got a bit of a surprise when these two great fast bowlers started nipping everything away off the seam. They were beating the outside edge for fun and Stewie could hardly lay a bat on it. England were skittled for 127 when the rain returned and sent them scurrying from the field once more.

As the players were hanging around waiting to go out again, Stewie ventured into the fast bowlers' corner to have a word and ask a question. 'Lads, can you tell me something?' he asked. 'When it comes to bowling, is it possible to be so precise as to know which way you move it off the seam? Last night Courtney and Curtly nipped everything back in at us and then this morning everything was nipping away. I didn't think it was possible to choose.'

One by one the bowlers answered. First, Angus Fraser told him that the aim of seam bowling is to get the seam upright so that it will do something off the pitch. If the ball wobbles a touch and goes one way or the other then so be it, but you won't know which way. That is left to how the ball hits the pitch. Chris Silverwood nodded in agreement, as did Dean Headley.

Ashley Cowan was there, too, and he said: 'That is the Holy Grail for a bowler. I've been able to control swing, but never seam, it's too unpredictable.'

Then came Caddick. 'I can control it,' he said. 'If I hold it this way, then it seams in and if I hold this other way, it seams away.'

All the other bowlers disagreed, but Caddick was having none of it. What started off as a discussion quickly escalated into a row, at which point Gus stood up and declared: 'I'm going to ask two blokes who know a thing or two about bowling and put an end to this.'

He went over and knocked on the West Indies dressing room.

'Excuse me, are Curtly and Courtney about? We've got a bit of a discussion going on and wondered if they could help.'

Invited to go and sit next to these two giant pace men, Gus put the question to them and together they gave the answer he was expecting. They try to put the ball on a good length with the seam upright, so if there is any movement then they get it. As for which way it goes, that is in the lap of the gods.

'Why do you want to know, Gus?' asked Walsh.

'Well, one of our bowlers reckons he can control which way the ball seams off the pitch.'

And in unison they both said, 'Caddick?!'

Back in the England dressing room Caddick was still sticking to his guns, but had been put back in his box by men with authority. By now the rain had stopped and it was time for England to head out into the field and for Caddick to show everyone what fantastic control he had.

Opening the batting for the West Indies were Clayton Lambert and Philo Wallace. Now, these two introduced Twenty20-style batting to Test cricket long before Chris Gayle came on the scene and they got the Windies off to an absolute flyer. They were going at about eight runs per over, if not more. The ball was pinging to the boundary and Caddick was coming in for a whole lot of punishment.

Out in the deep, Gus was running around like a blue-arsed fly trying to stop the ball and, as he crossed in front of the pavilion in pursuit once more, Courtney poked his head out of the window of the dressing room and shouted: 'Hey, Gus! God knows what the score would be if he didn't know which way it was seaming!'

David 'Bumble' Lloyd is the 'mad professor' of English cricket. He loves the game more than anyone I know. His passion for Lancashire and England as a player and then a coach knew no bounds and now, as a respected commentator offering views on the game, his insight is full of his love for it. He is, however, quite mad. There is rarely a dull moment in the Sky commentary box when Bumble is around, and without a mic in his hand he is even more mischievous. You might be reading through one of the excellent cricket articles in the Daily Mirror *when all of a sudden, from nowhere, Jim Bowen declares, 'Super! Smashing! Great!' Only it isn't Jim Bowen; it's Bumble with his* Bullseye *toy blaring out catchphrases. He is a lovable menace.*

DAVID LLOYD – THINKING OUTSIDE THE BOX

I'm sure his Royal Highness the 'Sir Loin of Beef' will have made a comment or two about me. Well, don't believe a word of it. He'll probably be trying to make me out to be the joker of the commentary box when the truth is there's only one menace in there, and that's him! Which one of us do you think offers commentators a bowl of spicy peanuts that he has sprinkled with extra tabasco and hot chilli powder? Beefy is just as much of a prankster now as when he was a lad in the dressing room.

The atmosphere in the commentary box is just like a cricket dressing room, only with slightly fewer mood swings. Sometimes I like to relax in the box when I'm not on and I would love to take my smart shoes off, but I daren't. They will only end up in the freezer like Nasser Hussain's did a couple of years ago. Beefy couldn't hide his delight when Nasser finally warmed them up enough to get his feet in, and had to put up with soggy, squelchy feet for the rest of the day. I tried to cheer Nasser up with a story about dodgy footwear, but he wasn't having any of it, he had a right sulk on. See what you think.

It was back in the early 1980s when David Steele had a spell playing for Derbyshire. He was a Northampton stalwart and returned there, but in between he had a time at Derby. Although known primarily as a batsman, and for his heroics against the Aussie pace attack in 1975, he also used to bowl a fair bit of left-arm spin and take wickets. I should know – he got me out a few times. Despite being a spinner he used to have a bit of trouble with no-balls, and in one particular game he was really struggling, bowling at least one per over.

Unsure what to do next, he came up with an ingenious plan during tea. With size eight feet, he felt he needed a bit more leeway when it came to getting something behind the line to stop the no-balls. He thought guys with size 11 or 12 feet were at an advantage because they had a greater margin of error. He had a word with their young tearaway fast bowler from Denmark, Ole Mortensen, and asked if he could borrow his boot. I say boot, singular, because he was only interested in his landing foot. So he went back out to field after tea with one normal sized boot and a giant floppy one on his right foot. He came back on to bowl, and with a shuffle and a jump he delivered . . . a no-ball.

You've got to give him credit for trying to think outside the box; it just didn't work. When I was a coach I tried all sorts of methods, in and out of the box, to try and get the most out of my teams. Sometimes they worked, sometimes they didn't. It makes me chuckle when I see how many staff and how much technology they use now, because when I was in charge I wasn't even allowed to buy a camcorder to video the players and review their technique – too expensive, apparently.

I must doff my cap to one of my favourite players, Wasim Akram, who was an absolute treat to work with. What a wonderful bowler, but he could also think outside the box when he wanted to. I was in charge up at Lancashire; we were getting ready for a match and the following day we would be setting off on the team coach. It was a club rule that when we had long away journeys, essentially any game south of Birmingham, we would travel as a team on the bus rather than making our own arrangements. Obviously, in exceptional circumstances people might be arriving from somewhere else, but if we were all in Manchester then we all got on the bus and travelled together to play.

I said: 'Right, lads, two o'clock for the bus tomorrow. Don't be late.'

Wasim replied: 'Not me, boss, I'm going by car.'

'No, Wasim,' I told him. 'You're up here with us, so there's no reason why you can't come on the bus. You know what the team rules are – if you're here, then you get on the bus.'

'Not me. I go by car,' he repeated.

'Come on, Wasim, you know how it goes.' I wasn't budging on this one. 'You've got to get on the bus with the rest of the team; we're all in it together. I can't have one rule for you and another for everyone else. You'll get on the bus tomorrow, won't you, there's a good lad.'

'Okay, I'll get on the bus,' he finally agreed.

Ian Botham

The next day at two the squad gathered at Old Trafford and they all, including Wasim, filed on to the coach, and we set off. We got out of Manchester and made our way on to the M6. After only five minutes rumbling down the motorway, the bus driver pulls over on to the hard shoulder and stops.

'What's going on? Have we broken down?' I enquire.

'No, he's getting off.' At which point Wasim Akram picks up a small bag, walks down the coach and, on the top step, turns to me and says:

'I get on bus like you say, now I get off bus.'

And with that he jumped into a car that had pulled up behind and whizzed off down the road. The rest of the lads were in stitches and, to be fair, I couldn't really argue with his thinking.

Playing cricket with Geoff Miller was a bit like going to work with John Bishop in your office – he just had a way of making you laugh even when you didn't want to. Having that sort of character, someone who gets everybody smiling, is vital to a dressing room. I used to get people going with things that I did but 'Dusty' was a man who got you chuckling with what he said, and he still does it now. Trust me, if you get the chance to go and hear him speak at a dinner or function, take that opportunity – you won't regret it. He was a handy spinning all-rounder with a knack for frustrating teams with the bat and taking vital wickets with the ball. He was a spinner I always felt we could rely on when he was in the England team; you knew what you were getting and it was good enough to outfox most batsmen. He has now carved out a terrific job as England's national selector. He understands what it takes to make it as an international cricketer, yet he is calm enough and sensible enough not to cast people aside too quickly and that has reaped huge rewards for the side. The days of the one-cap wonder have been largely numbered under him and that is a good thing. Despite all that, I still don't know where Darren Pattinson came from and I make sure to bring it up whenever I see him.

GEOFF MILLER – THE ENTERTAINER

A wonderful game played by wonderful people, in the main. That is what cricket looks like to me and I've been lucky enough to have been involved in the game at all levels for a lifetime. It has given me so much and hopefully I've treated it with respect and love in return.

I've also learnt a huge amount from the game and the people in it, none more so than Ian Terence Botham. We shared an England dressing room for several years and were good mates throughout. I got to witness some of the most memorable things on a cricket field thanks to him and although I might not have been able to do some of the things he did, he still taught me a thing or two. For example, we were playing in a Test match in Sydney during the 1978/79 series, so this was well before the legend of Beefy was born in 1981. But even then he had a twinkle in his eye and an air of mischievousness about him.

On day one we were struggling a little bit. Boycott, Brearley and Randall had all come and gone inside the first hour and a half and we hadn't even posted 50. Beefy was the next man in and, as we sat in the dressing room, David Gower got out and it was time for our all-rounder to dig us out of a hole.

The captain, an intelligent man who understood the game down to its core, turned to Beefy and said: 'Now, Ian, you can see the trouble we're in, so just bat according to the situation. If we can frustrate their bowlers a little bit we might just be able to post a score here. Bat according to the situation.'

With that, Beefy got up and said: 'Yes, skipper, I understand, skipper. The situation needs careful attention. I've played several times for my country and rest assured I will play accordingly.'

He picked up his bat and gloves and walked out the door.

A second later, the door opened again and he popped his head back in. 'Just one other thing, though, skipper. There are forty thousand punters who have bought tickets to watch this game, and, well, they need entertaining as well, don't they?'

And before Brears could object, Beefy was gone and jogging his way down the steps on to the field. 'Oh, Ian . . .' was the response as we then all took our seats to see the outcome of this tussle.

Back then we still weren't quite sure how good this young man would prove to be, but we got another glimpse of it as he somehow stayed true to both masters. He batted for almost two and a half hours – longer than anyone else managed – and struck a seemingly dominant 59 that included seven thumping fours. And lo and behold, we actually got a score of some description by reaching 152 all out. It shouldn't have been enough but we clawed our way back into the game thanks to Derek Randall's 150. We needed runs and we needed to take time out of the game due to our first innings collapse, so who do you think then batted and faced 88 balls for a grand total of six runs? Why, Beefy, of course. It was a great lesson to learn. Entertaining the crowd is as fundamental to the game as helping your team win, but just because you can do something, doesn't mean you have to if it is not in the interests of the team. It is because of that outlook that we all loved him.

There were times, though, when everything wasn't necessarily hunky-dory between us, but these would be momentary disagreements that blew over as fast as they came. One such time was when I was playing for Derbyshire against him at Taunton, and it was one of those long days in the field for me in which I bowled almost unchanged from one end all day.

It was hot, sweaty and I was knackered. Still, I kept coming in to bowl, hoping that one of them would turn and I might sneak another wicket. Kim Barnett was captain and he just wanted me to bowl over after over, and by this stage I had taken five for

170. Colin Dredge came in and first ball he reverse lapped me for four so I'm five for 174. The next ball he hit hard and straight and it landed right in the middle of the Somerset changing room. In those days they had a full-size snooker table in their dressing room. The ball has clattered into the room and, as I'm waiting to get it back, Botham has come out on to the balcony and shouted at the top of his voice: 'ONE HUNDRED AND EIGHTY!!'

And with that he's lobbed a red snooker ball from on high down on to the outfield and said, 'Why don't you try bowling with this – he won't be able to hit that one so far!'

By now I've got my pecker up and I'm not having anyone give me that kind of stick – Botham or otherwise. So I ran after that snooker ball, picked it up and launched it hard and far into the river by the ground, telling him to, 'Try and pocket that one!' He simply laughed and went back into the dressing room – and poor old muggins here just had to keep on bowling.

Cricketers who can excite the public are a rare breed, but they are the ones who are loved the most. For all the joy that comes from winning, when people turn up to watch sport they want to be entertained and Eoin Morgan is a player who guarantees entertainment. He hits the ball hard and into unusual areas. He is clinical, he is unorthodox and he gives punters value for money. Who wouldn't want to see him reverse sweep an Aussie bowler for six? Born and raised in Ireland, he made the right choice in coming over to play for England because Test match cricket is where he belongs. One day that might become a reality for Ireland but, until then, I'm glad we've got his services.

EOIN MORGAN – LONG TRAIN RUNNING

There are one or two recurring nightmares that cricketers have, only I've experienced both in real life. Back in 2006 I was playing for Middlesex against Sussex at Lord's in a Pro40 game and got taught a very valuable lesson about communication. I turned up, looked for my name on the team sheet and there it was, as per usual, down at No. 6. That was my spot as a young player making his way in the game; I was learning my trade.

We won the toss and chose to bat so I settled into my normal routine. I like to have a cup of tea, sit and have a look at a paper or a magazine and then, when the first wicket falls, think about changing into my kit. When the second wicket falls I get changed into the right clothes. When the third wicket falls I put on my protective gear and my pads, ready to make that move down the steps and on to the field when the fourth wicket goes down. It is the same for No. 6 batsmen the world over and never usually causes a problem.

On this day, Paul Weekes, our opener, fell instantly, second ball, so Owais Shah went in. He lasted just five balls, so I had to get changed in the second over.

I was mid-change when John Emburey, our coach, came into the dressing room and shouted, 'Morgs! What the f**king f**k do you think you're doing in here, you're in!'

Occasionally Embers could be a bit of a joker and I thought he was having me on. So I stood there completely naked, with nothing but a jockstrap in hand ready to get my kit on.

'Don't muck about now, Embers,' I said.

At that point our captain, Ben Hutton, put his hands to his head and said: 'Oh, crap, sorry Morgs, I didn't tell you – you're batting at four today!'

This was my worst nightmare. Due into bat and being stark naked. Normally, in my nightmare I am walking out to bat like this in front of a huge crowd, so at least I was spared that part, but my heart was going 19 to the dozen anyway. By now Owais has reached the gate at the pavilion and I've got three minutes to get dressed, get my pads on and get out to the middle to face the next ball. No chance.

Thankfully, Sussex were oblivious to the problems in our dressing room and weren't exactly ready to appeal for timed out. Also, our No. 5 that day, Scott Styris, was further along the road than me and he unselfishly walked out to bat. After about 20 minutes it became clear that he was struggling with a back problem and had to retire hurt. Things were going from bad to worse for us. At least I was ready to bat this time and walked out to the middle confidently and took guard.

After what had gone before I couldn't believe what happened next. I played a big drive and out of nowhere my back went, too! I had to retire hurt, just like Scott. If it wasn't for Ed Smith's 87 we'd have been sunk already. As it was we lost the match anyway, using two substitute fielders in the process. It was not a day I cared to remember too much.

However, the one saving grace was that at least I turned up.

Fast forward to 2012 and another nightmare that taught me about back-up plans. I was due to play for Middlesex in a CB40 match against Lancashire at Old Trafford and it was a big game because we were pushing for a semi-final spot. With the game being a day/nighter starting at 4.40 p.m. I thought I would take the train up rather than drive. It is much quicker and easier and I wouldn't have to worry about anything en route.

I got to Euston for my 10.30 train and sat patiently waiting for it to move. It remained on the platform for 20 minutes before there was an announcement that someone had fallen on to the track and therefore the train on this line was cancelled. I had two options. Either I could go home and get the car, which would make it touch-and-go as to whether I got there in time for the warm-up; or I could go to King's Cross where there was a train stopping at Leeds, from where I could easily get to Manchester in good time. I chose the train.

We set off okay and I telephoned Angus Fraser, our director of cricket, to let him know what was going on and he was happy with it. As the train got into the Midlands it started slowing down to a crawl. It seemed to stop at every little station and take ages to move on again. Somewhere just north of Nottingham there was another announcement. This train was now not stopping at Leeds, but instead was heading to York and then on to Durham.

A little nervous, I asked how easy it would be to get from York to Manchester. Not a problem, the guard told me.

Imagine my horror when the train reached York and then refused to stop. Off it trundled towards Durham. Nightmare number two was in full swing. I called my agent in a bit of a panic and was looking for some advice and support. The best he could come up with was, 'I'm glad I don't have to phone Gus.'

I put it off for as long as I could, but with the clock ticking I dialled the number. 'Hi, Gus.'

'All right, Morgs, you in Manchester now?' he asked.

'Erm, not quite. I'm actually in Durham.'

'You f**king what?! How bloody stupid are you?'

I wanted to tell him it wasn't really my fault, but I knew that wouldn't cut it. I had a responsibility to be at the ground by a certain time and I wasn't going to make it. He had every right to have a go, and he did.

I got on a train from Durham back to York and then from York to Manchester and arrived at the ground two overs into the game. Middlesex were batting and rain had stopped play, so theoretically they could have named me in the side and then I could have batted. But Gus couldn't take that risk, what with me being halfway between Durham and York and, based on recent experience, not really sure whether or not the train would actually stop at York. I watched the game with the rest of the squad and thought of what might have been, as we lost by seven wickets.

The next two games were both away, to Essex and to Gloucestershire. Needless to say, I drove to both.

It is unsurprising that the very best sportsmen in their chosen arena could often have made it just as successfully in another sport. The skills that you need in one sphere can be easily transplanted, whether it is pace, agility or hand–eye coordination, these are the things that all great sportsmen share. In Hugh Morris's case, he could just as easily have been a Welsh wizard on the rugby field as he was the bard of Glamorgan County Cricket Club. Rugby's loss was cricket's gain, as he went on to reach the pinnacle of the game, playing Test cricket for England. Rest assured, though, that if Wales could have played Test cricket he would have done it for them. Instead, he gave his heart and soul to Glamorgan and took them to a Sunday League title as captain and played a crucial role in their County Championship win as a determined opening batsman. He took the same fight that he showed on the field into his battle with throat cancer, which he won. Now he is giving something back and showing what a versatile man he is as the England and Wales Cricket Board's managing director of cricket.

HUGH MORRIS – BOWLING LIKE THE WIND FROM THE WINDIES

They say you never forget your debut, and to this day I can remember it as if it were yesterday. Receiving my Test cap and jumper in the post, trying it on for size and then meeting up with the team beforehand, it is all part of the ritual that gets you to the point where you cross the ropes and go into battle for your nation.

However, it was actually my second Test that sticks in my mind far more than my first, not only because I scored more runs, but also because there was one sight that signified I was playing Test cricket more than any other. It was 1991 and I had been scoring runs for fun for Glamorgan. I had been the first to 1,000 runs that season and the year before, and in 1990 I scored a record 2,276 runs for the county, so I was feeling in terrific form and felt my chance with England would come. A tour to Sri Lanka the previous winter with England A showed that I was on the selectors' radar but, like every other cricketer in the land, I desperately wanted to play Test cricket.

At the start of the series between England and the West Indies Graham Gooch and Mike Atherton were England's opening pair, so I was left waiting for a chance to try and force my way in. That chance came in the fourth Test when Robin Smith was injured and they called me up, with Athers ready to drop to No. 3 and everyone shuffling down one. I was actually relieved they called me up because a week earlier I had played against the Windies in a tour match at Swansea, where I had picked up the only pair of my career.

Thankfully, they still wanted to give me a chance so here I was in Birmingham, ready to play in my first Test match. We were level 1–1 in the series. Goochie won the toss and batted. Out I walked with him to face up to the Windies pace attack, heart beating like the clappers, but thrilled to be part of the action. I got three in the first innings and not as many as that in the second, as we lost the game to go 2–1 down.

I honestly thought that was it, my one chance to play Test cricket and I'm going to end up in the one-cap wonders hall of fame. Robin Smith was fit to play in the final Test match so he was bound to come back in. Only he came in for Allan Lamb rather than me, so I was clear to play in another Test. I think that sense of relief actually helped settle me down a bit because I enjoyed my second Test experience much more than my first.

We turned up at The Oval needing to win the game to square the series. It was Viv Richards' last game, which made it even more special for me, and I'll tell you why in a moment. It was also Malcolm Marshall's last game, so there was a real air of anticipation and we all felt it.

We won the toss again and batted. The Oval pitch was as hard as granite and quick as lightning. So, with half an hour to go, I'm upstairs in the changing room putting on my pads, my thigh pad, my chest guard, my arm guard, my box and any other bit of protective equipment I can find. The bell rings and it is time to get out there. When the umpires walk out there is a big roar and when Viv leads out his West Indies team there is an even bigger roar. Goochie taps me on the shoulder and says, 'Come on, Hughie, let's go and do this.'

The nerves are there at the surface and the biggest roar of the lot for the two of us has sent a shiver down my spine. Halfway out to the middle I manage to catch my breath and compose myself, and at the crease I'm actually feeling all right. I'm at the non-striker's end and there he was, all six foot seven of him and the most feared fast bowler in the world at the time – Curtly Ambrose. He is marking his run-up and I'm thinking, Christ, he looks bigger than he did when he was bowling for Northamptonshire.

Now, I'd faced Curtly lots of times before in county cricket and I knew what a special bowler he was, but you could always tell whether he was really up for it or not. He used to give a little shake of the wrist just before he delivered the ball and you knew that if he shook it once he was maybe a bit tired and wasn't really interested. If he shook it twice, then he was probably holding it back because it was a flat pitch. If he shook it three times, then he was getting interested; and if he shook it four times, then you'd better watch out because he meant business.

So, he's at the end of his mark, the clock strikes 11 and the umpire says, 'Play!' He charges in and I think, I'd better watch the shakes. Up goes the wrist – one ... two ... three ... four ... five! And he lets the ball go.

It pitches two-thirds of the way down and goes screeching past Goochie's nose. Jeff Dujon, the keeper, is standing 30 yards back. He leaps into the air to take this catch one-handed above his head. My knees are knocking and the nerves that had disappeared are back with a vengeance. Curtly turns around to walk back to his mark and he is grinning from ear to ear. Now, Curtly is not a man of many words, but as he passes me he turns to look at me and says, 'Have a nice day, man.'

FIT FOR PURPOSE

Some players were born to lead, others learn how to take the reins and others really shouldn't be left in charge of anything more than ordering the wine. Needless to say, I fell into the last of these categories and the less said about my record as England captain the better!

There were one or two mitigating circumstances surrounding my leadership, such as coming up against the West Indies in their pomp on my first tour in charge. However, the Ashes summer of 1981 showed just where my talents lay. I was responsible for imposing one of the more bizarre rules as captain, which under the current regime would never be entertained, let alone accepted. We were in the Caribbean, Barbados to be precise, and after a few weeks on tour I noticed that one of our players was looking a little lacklustre towards the end of each day.

Graham Gooch was as committed a cricketer as you are likely to find, but his chat in the evenings at team meetings or team dinners was appalling, especially when he was face down in his flying fish and green banana. I thought that it was probably the heat that had got to him, which is why he kept falling asleep at the table, but as it turned out there was another reason, as I discovered for myself.

Returning to the hotel one morning as the sun was coming up I noticed Goochie milling about in the lobby, looking a little shifty. I thought that he must have had a big night himself and was worried about spotting the captain on his way back to his room in the early hours. It was never in my nature to stop a bloke from having fun, as long as he was producing it on the field, so I went over to him to tell him not to worry and that it would be our little secret. It turned out that Goochie was not just coming in, but actually heading out for an early morning run! This is what he'd been doing all tour and he was off to pound the streets of Bridgetown.

That day we trained as per usual and then that night we were out in St Lawrence Gap, at a bar called the Ship, and midway through the evening Goochie fell asleep again. Well, enough was enough. I couldn't have my players so tired before a game that they were unable even to stay awake for the whole day.

At the next team meeting I got up and told the group that I'd heard that some players had been going for early morning runs and it was making them tired, so from that point on all extra-early morning runs were banned. There wasn't too much of an argument from most of the squad, but Goochie's commitment to fitness bordered on the obsessive and I had to stop him.

Where our opinions really differed, though, was the reason behind my decision. I wanted Goochie to be fresh for the action. I wanted him getting tired playing the game and scoring runs, not beforehand. There was being fit and then there was overdoing it, and I thought he was not going to give himself the best chance of doing a job for the team if he was already knackered by the time he got out to the middle. Goochie thought I just wanted him to stop so that he would be more fun on a night out. That wasn't my main aim but of course it wouldn't hurt team spirit if we didn't all fall asleep in the middle of a meal.

Paul Nixon is one of the game's great characters, who made sure he wrung every last drop of ability out of his frame before finally calling it a day in 2011. As a wicket-keeper he is bound to be different, but he took this to the extreme. I've never met a more energetic, talkative, obsessive, mad and enthusiastic cricketer. He just loved the game, morning, noon and night, and it came across. If you played against him he would annoy the hell out of you, especially when you batted, and if you played with him you would be grateful he was on your side but you'd still probably want him to shut up! A stalwart for Leicestershire in two spells at the club, I'm delighted he managed to accomplish his dream of playing for England, when he made a huge difference to the one-day series that followed the 2006/07 Ashes tour. I don't think England would have come anywhere near winning that series if it hadn't been for his whole new level of encouragement after the 5–0 Test defeat. It was his finest hour.

PAUL NIXON – DRESSING-ROOM ARGY-BARGY

In a cricket dressing room you have to be mindful of the different personalities found there, because you never get 11 guys who have the same outlook on life and like the same things. The obvious differences can be spotted in the music people listen to and what gets played on the team stereo, or the food and drink they prefer. Some people crave peace and quiet, others like hustle and bustle and a bit of noise. It is why you get clashes and why sometimes the best place to be in a cricket dressing room is out in the middle, because that is the only time when everyone is doing whatever they can to pull the team in the same direction. There are rarely any issues on the field because runs, wickets and catches are the only currency that matter.

Clashes occasionally bubbled over in my time as a professional cricketer, sometimes due to a build-up of things and at other times it just took a spark to set one off. Normally these would all be sorted out there and then and you move on. One such occasion was the morning of a game back in the early 1990s, and the guys in the dressing room were getting themselves ready in their own way.

Gordon Parsons was a giant of a man and you didn't really mess with him too much because there was always the fear that he could break you in half like a twig. He liked things done a certain way and that included a cup of coffee so big it was more like a pint than a cup. He had this giant mug and would sit in the dressing room working his way through it, to get him up and ready for the day. He would also arrive at the ground already changed and in his whites, so that once he was ready for action there was no faffing around getting into his kit.

Anyway, this particular morning there were a few young lads in the dressing room at the same time as Gordon, and they were making a fair old racket playing with a tennis ball.

Gordon turned to them and said, 'Do you mind, lads? I'm trying to get a bit of peace before the game so can you take it outside or quieten down?'

It was a bit chilly out, so the lads carried on playing in the dressing room, and inevitably the noise level rose again. Gordon hadn't got through much of his coffee yet and was getting a bit hacked off, so with a bit more menace he said, 'Look, lads, will you stop playing with that bloody tennis ball or I will stick it some place where the sun doesn't shine.'

At this point, frustrated that their game was over, a young player called Andrew Roseberry threw the ball in anger against the wall. He watched in dismay and then in horror as the ball bounced off the wall, hit the next wall and then landed perfectly in Gordon's mug, spilling scalding-hot coffee all over him and all over his whites, including his old woollen Leicestershire jumper which needed more than one dry-clean afterwards. I have never seen anyone move as fast as Andrew did to get out of the dressing room and on to the outfield to run away from him. The rest of us were howling with laughter, but Gordon wasn't and he made sure Andrew never played with a tennis ball in the changing room again.

It was all good-natured, though, in the end. Similarly, in Durban on a pre-season tour there was a friendly dust-up between Ian Sutcliffe and Adrian Pearson, our off spinner, which could have ended much worse. Sutty had an Oxford Blue for boxing and was actually offered terms to turn professional, but he opted for cricket instead. He was still a very handy boxer, though, and at the end of a training session he asked the lads who fancied a sparring session. Adrian put up his hand, despite being the most gangly and awkward-looking boxer you have ever seen. Six foot five and as thin as a drainpipe, he was hardly Mike Tyson.

Anyway, the pair of them stripped down to their jockstraps and Sutty said, 'I'll tie my hands behind my back and you can have the gloves so you won't hit me.' Off they went, with Adrian lurching at him and groping thin air, Sutty bobbing and weaving like a pro and getting out of the way with ease. This went on for a couple of minutes before Adrian went for a big hook. Leaning back, Sutty tripped, lost his footing and went careering back towards the drinks table. There were 30 half-pint glasses on the table with squash and water in them and Sutty landed square on top of them. It was carnage and Adrian only narrowly managed to avoid falling on top of him. His hands were tied so he couldn't break his fall and he smashed every last glass. We all ran over to him fearing the worst, expecting blood to be pouring out of his back. To this day I don't know how, but he got up, glass everywhere, and not a scratch on him. It was unbelievable.

However, not every dressing room bust-up is that good-natured. Back in the 1990s we were playing in a festival game against Yorkshire and James Whittaker scored a hundred. Winston Benjamin was really annoyed about this because he felt that Jimmy, as a Yorkshireman, tried harder in the games against Yorkshire than he did in other championship games. It wasn't the case, but he had a bee in his bonnet about it.

There is one thing you should understand about Winston Benjamin – he doesn't like anyone touching his kit. He likes it just so and no one is allowed to touch it. Anyway, Jimmy was not having any of the accusation and kicked Winston's kit. Benjy was so incensed by this that he grabbed his bat and went to hit Jimmy with it. Peter Willey leapt out of the way and Les Taylor, ex-army and strong as an ox, jumped on Benjy and got him in a headlock. 'Are you okay, Benjy? Have you calmed down?'

'Yeah, yeah, yeah, I'm good,' said Benjy.

He let him up and Benjy shot straight for Jimmy, so Les had to jump on him again and squeeze him to the floor, saying,

'Benjy, you can't do this, man, leave him, leave it. I can't let you up unless you stop.' By now there were quite a few people watching the drama because the doors open wide at Scarborough, so we closed them and kept him inside. Benjy was such a terrific athlete we needed a couple of other lads to sit on him and stop him from getting up. We had to restrain him for 15 minutes before he finally calmed down. If we hadn't, I'm certain he would have knocked Jimmy out with a cricket bat because he was so angry.

That was a dressing room on the edge. We were going through a bad patch and everything had built up to that moment, and if it wasn't for Les we could have had a horrible story on our hands.

Being the son of a famous cricketer is hard, just ask my lad Liam, but being the son AND nephew of two of your country's finest players must come with a health warning. Shaun Pollock had a lot to live up to when he decided to try and make cricket his career, but he didn't only match the feats of his dad and uncle, Graeme and Peter Pollock, he exceeded them through his ability and longevity. As a fast bowling all-rounder, Shaun is a man after my own heart and he was a fearsome competitor. Playing, as he did, in the immediate aftermath of South Africa's reintroduction to world sport also came with a certain amount of pressure and he rose to the challenge magnificently. Knowing him off the field as I do, I can't think of a more genuine and likeable gentleman involved in the game. He was the perfect ambassador for his country. On the field he was one half of a terrifying opening bowling partnership. For Pakistan's Wasim and Waqar, or the Windies' Ambrose and Walsh, read South Africa's Donald and Pollock. If you were a batsman during the late 1990s and 2000s, the chances are Shaun Pollock got you out. That is just a fact.

SHAUN POLLOCK – RUNNERS AND RIDERS

World Cups have not been particularly kind to South Africa since we had our first taste back in 1992 and were asked to score 22 runs from one ball in the semi-final against England. That came about as a result of some antiquated rain-delay rules that made a mockery of the game at times. I can still remember watching Chris Lewis run in to bowl that ball and Brian McMillan with no option but to pat it hopelessly back down the ground. It wasn't quite the Trevor Chappell pea-roller but the conclusion was still the same – an impossible chance of victory.

From there South Africa have flirted with the tournament on several occasions, daring to suggest that we might win it, but never quite getting over the line. It is a source of huge disappointment for many of us who played that we often felt like we had a talented enough team to go on and win the cup, only to have fate or, more accurately, our own failings to blame for not getting the prize we all wanted.

In 2003, on home soil, we really should have done better, but again the rain played its part. The old rules had long gone and we were now using the Duckworth–Lewis method, which is a much fairer way of finding a winner. The only issue with it is that you must learn how to read the charts before sending instructions out to your team-mates. In our case, we thought the numbers on the sheet were the totals to win a rain-affected match, whereas actually they were the scores to be level and you actually needed one more in order to win. I had to take the can for that one as captain, but you can be sure I know how to read a D–L chart now!

The World Cup that sticks out in my mind, though, is the one in 1999, and not just because of what happened on the field. We met Australia in the semi-final at Edgbaston and were playing the best one-day cricket of our lives. Australia were hugely impressive, too, and the feeling was that whoever won this particular semi-final would go on to lift the trophy, which is what happened.

The drama that got us to that point was practically unbearable. From Herschelle Gibbs's dropped catch to reprieve Steve Waugh when they were wobbling, to the run chase that turned into a nightmare, and then back and forth again. The moment everyone remembers, though, was that run-out. Lance Klusener and Allan Donald together needed just one run to win the game. It should have been so straightforward, but cricket never is. I would have put my mortgage on them getting us over the line, but in a moment of excitement all rational thought went out of the window and, in an almost comical bit of cricket, AD was run out by a country mile and Australia had won. That in itself was extremely hard to take. There was no blame attached to those guys at all, it really shouldn't have come down to them, but that is the beauty and the cruelty of sport.

After that crushing blow, I went back to South Africa for a break. Every year there is a showpiece horse race in Durban and I thought I would go and watch it with some friends. I bumped into a lot of people during that day who were very supportive and who commiserated with me over our World Cup exit; and, of course, there were a few people who had a bit of a laugh and a joke about it as well.

One bloke I knew, who was very knowledgeable on the horses, came and had a chat with me and we went over the semi-final. At the end of it I said to him, 'Anyway, what about this race? What is your tip for me today?'

He looked at me and smiled, 'The only tip I've got for you is don't back No. 10, he's no good at running.'

I knew exactly what he meant. AD wore No. 10 in our semi-final and that run-out was going to follow him for some time yet. Even though this guy was joking, I took note and backed another horse instead. I then wondered whether in some way I was going against my old friend AD. I kept thinking I should have backed No. 10 as a show of support for our own No. 10. I didn't and had to watch as El Picha romped home in first place and taught me a very costly lesson!

I told the boys the next time I saw them and they all mocked me for not backing him. I wasn't going to make the same mistake twice, so the following year I backed El Picha even though horses almost never win the Durban Cup back-to-back. And, guess what, he won again. It only took a year, but El Picha played his part in getting me over a World Cup semi-final defeat.

Derek Pringle was one of the first all-rounders to be unfairly tagged with the 'New Ian Botham' moniker – and I was still playing! 'Suggsy' and me go way back and had many a great day on the field and night off it together. He's my kind of guy – not one to conform to the status quo. He's an original thinker, a clever bloke who looks at the game and the world a little differently to others and revels in that fact. As a cricketer he was hugely talented and in particular as a bowler very skilful. His performance in the World Cup final of 1992 should have been a man-of-the-match display – if only there had been DRS at the time he struck Javed Miandad on the pads. His love of music and wine make him an interesting bloke to talk to, and in his subsequent career as the Daily Telegraph *cricket correspondent he has not been afraid to voice an opinion within their pages. Whether you agree or disagree doesn't matter; at least he will get you thinking.*

DEREK PRINGLE – PUTTING A NAME TO A FACE

The first thing you need to know about the great Essex stalwart Keith Fletcher is that his memory isn't his strength. Despite being the best captain I ever played under he would regularly get mixed up with names and faces. For many a year he would call me 'Pritch' and he would refer to our team-mate Paul Prichard as 'Pring'. Of course, we knew what he meant and it was all part of his character.

Back in 1987 we were on the road, playing Worcestershire relatively early in the season, or at least early in the season back in those days. And it being late May there was usually a bit of weather around, and the seam bowlers would generally fill their boots in classic swinging and seaming conditions. We began our three-day county match first, with the Sunday League game to follow the next day, before returning to the championship match.

It was a bit of an on-off day, with the clouds constantly threatening, and Worcestershire had reached 106 for two when the heavens opened around lunchtime and finished play for the day.

During rain delays, players would search for things to do to occupy their time; some would sleep, some would read the papers or check out the racing form, and others would play cards. There was a bit of a card school in the Worcestershire dressing room and our latest signing, Geoff Miller, went and joined in the fun. With Ian Botham in their dressing room during the late 1980s there was always likely to be a famous face or two lurking nearby, and on that day Eric Clapton was hanging out with his mate.

Not content with being one of the world's greatest guitarists he also knew his way around a card table. When 'Dusty' Miller came back into our dressing room, it was clear he hadn't had the rub of the green while Eric had. He was muttering something along the lines of, 'Bloody typical, it's not as if the bloke needs the money.'

Clearly sensing that it had been a bit of a tough day for the players who had lost their money to him, Eric offered to do something to make up for it. He said he would put on a private gig for the Worcestershire and Essex players at Beefy's local pub, if he could find an amplifier to play with. He called up the local music shop and asked whether they had the specific amplifier he was looking for and the assistant said: 'Yes, we've got one left.'

'Great,' said Eric. 'What time do you open until?'

'6 p.m.'

'Okay, well, I'll swing by at 5.45 and pick it up. Can you put it aside for me, please?'

'Well, what if someone comes in before then and wants to buy it?'

'Don't sell it to them, put it aside for me and I promise I'll be in to get it before you close.'

'Okay, then. What's your name?'

'Eric Clapton.'

'Do you think I was born yesterday, mate?'

And with that he put down the phone. Luckily for us, Eric did swing by the shop. He gave the assistant the surprise of his life and, thankfully, the amp was still there, so he could bring it with him to the local pub. All the Essex players were there and a few locals, too, but not many of the Worcestershire team – clearly this sort of thing happened all the time for the team-mates of Beefy.

After a few drinks Eric got up and started playing. It was brilliant. An intimate gig, with everybody enjoying the tunes. Inevitably, word got around that a world-famous musician was playing at the pub and the numbers started to swell. Soon after, it got a bit too rowdy for Eric's liking and he stopped playing, much to the frustration of the crowd. They booed his departure from the makeshift stage, but the performance was over.

The next day, he was back at New Road and he had a face like thunder. He was clearly not happy at being booed the night before, or so you would think. As it turned out, his upset stemmed from something more costly. Beefy had asked to take the wheels of his Ferrari that morning and reluctantly Eric let him drive it to the ground. 'He scratched the side of my car on the gates to the ground!' wailed Eric. 'The bloody paint job is going to cost four grand alone!' Far from winning money at the card game, this was turning into an expensive few days for the Cream star.

The players were by now turning their attentions to the Sunday League game that was about to start. After batting first, Essex made 202 in our 40 overs, with yours truly smiting what I thought was a useful 40 not out. That knock was put into perspective when Beefy went out there and did what he was best at – winning games of cricket. He absolutely smashed it, with one of Hugh Page's deliveries virtually destroying a tea tent at the back of the ground. Beefy finished his big-hitting innings 125 not out, as Worcestershire won the game by nine wickets with over eight overs spare. It was a shellacking.

The Essex dressing room was a quiet place after the game but we had to have a chat about it, and with Fletch and Graham Gooch in charge we weren't expecting any pulled punches.

Just then Eric walked into our dressing room and, being a bit of a chilled-out rock 'n' roller, he said, 'Hey, guys, don't let the game get you down. Don't worry, be happy.'

At which point Fletch turned to him and said, 'Excuse me, Ernie, but could you give us a minute, please.' And without even mentioning the obvious error, Eric just nodded and quietly left the room.

Paul Prichard piped up: 'What did you just call him?'

Fletch replied: 'Don't you know who that is? It's Ernie Clapham, he's a world-famous guitarist.'

At which point the room erupted with laughter, and that is how Eric Clapton was forever known as Ernie Clapham in the Essex dressing room.

*Each step on the road to being an England cricketer is about trying
to be the best in whatever level of cricket you're playing. First, it is
being the best in your school or club team, then it is about being
the best in your county team, then the best in England and, finally,
the target has to be the best in the world. Obviously, very few
manage to get there but much of the fun is in the attempt. In the
case of Matt Prior, he has done it. In an era of brilliant wicket-
keeper batsmen, with Adam Gilchrist setting the benchmark, Prior
has emerged as the best in the business at what he does. He scores
runs, takes catches and stumpings and, crucially, is the heartbeat
of this England Test team. He is a big reason why they reached
No. 1 in the world, and when they get back there it will be with
him behind the stumps, rabbiting away with the authority of a
sergeant major.*

MATT PRIOR – YOU'VE GOT TO ACCENTUATE THE POSITIVES

I think being a professional sportsman is all about positivity.
You've got to think positively, be positive and help your
team-mates in a positive way. It might sound a bit like psycho-
babble, but if you stop and think for a moment you can see why,
in our environment, it is better to be that way.

When things go well it produces feelings of positivity and
confidence, and that is what you then feed off to keep the good
times rolling. The flip side of the coin is that defeat and poor
form create a negative situation, which can bring you down.

You need to try to let that go so you can get back to performing at your best again. Of course, this is not the only guide to success and failure – the thousands of hours of hard work and sacrifice have a fair bit to do with it as well, but every little one per cent improvement helps.

Sometimes in this country we can be a little down on our sportsmen and women, even when they are trying to do amazing things, and there is no doubt we're a bit wary of too much positivity. Call it *'EastEnders* syndrome', if you like. Nothing like a miserable storyline to keep the viewers hooked!

Things are a lot different in other parts of the world and the award for the most positive nation surely has to go to the USA. The American people are so unbelievably friendly and upbeat that you wonder how anything gets them down. Watching sport on television out there you just get the sense that they only want to deal with the good stuff, and that they leave all the poor performances and difficult results behind them. For an English cricketer it still takes some getting used to.

Not too long ago, a group of us were over in Las Vegas for a short break following a demanding period in the schedules. It was our chance to let our hair down. Now, you'll all be familiar with the rule 'what happens in Vegas stays in Vegas', but one thing I will share with you is about this positive attitude and how it can help. There were six of us in the group, all England cricketers, and we'd had a pretty heavy night out before heading out on to the golf course the following morning. We were a shambles. We looked terrible, were shuffling about talking nonsense and generally making a nuisance of ourselves.

It was a typically immaculate American golf course that upheld all the finest traditions of the game. There was a beautiful oak-panelled clubhouse and everything about the place was pristine; we, on the other hand, were not. We made our way out towards the putting green and some of the members warming up looked less than impressed. About 15 minutes later, it was our turn to tee off and, just as we got to the first tee box, we noticed the course manager driving towards us in a golf buggy. We were sure that one of the members had been offended and had reported us to the club in an attempt to get us chucked off the course. We all knew what was coming and braced ourselves.

The buggy didn't quite reach us and instead swerved off to the left. As it passed by, the manager leaned out towards us and yelled: 'Hey, guys! Go out there and get me some BIRD-IES! YEAH!!' We all turned and looked at each other, and automatically responded: 'YEAH!! We got some with your name on!'

It completely took us by surprise and it immediately picked us all up. We went on to have a terrific day's golf, one that we will never forget. Back in the clubhouse after the round, the only thing we were talking about was how positive the Americans were and how it lifted us when we needed it. So now, if things are drifting along out in the middle, don't be perplexed if you hear me over the stump mic asking for our bowlers to: 'Go get me some birdies!!'

I try to take this positive attitude into every game we play and there have been clear examples where it has worked, but at other times you just have to accept that no amount of enthusiasm will hide a shocker. Ahead of the 2010/11 Ashes series, everyone was feeling pretty good about our chances and, after winning or drawing all of our first three practice games, we knew we were on the right track. Still, when it came to Ashes cricket, we knew it would be much tougher.

The first Test was in Brisbane and from the start we were determined to be positive, both in what we said and in our actions. When we arrived in the dressing room on the first morning, I took my place on one of the long chairs and Stuart Broad set up next to me on my left. I turned to my right and there was Andrew Strauss, the England captain. I thought to myself, This is a high-quality bench. I've got our leader and inspiration, Straussy, on one side, and a world-class all-rounder, who's just reeled off a ton against Pakistan at Lord's, on the other. When Straussy came back from the toss and told us we were batting, I turned to them both and said: 'Look at this bench, boys, we couldn't have a more solid trio here. Runs are to be had, today is going to be a good day with you either side of me.'

They both agreed and I know it might seem a bit silly, but that sort of thing is important between team-mates, always backing each other up and reaffirming positive ideas. The game got underway, with Straussy and Alastair Cook walking out to bat. Three balls later, the captain was walking back, gone for a duck. Never mind, these things happen. Australia took wickets reasonably steadily during the day until Peter Siddle, on his birthday, got on a bit of a roll and took an impressive hat-trick. His wickets number two and number three were yours truly and Stuart Broad. The atmosphere and noise were incredible and that Ashes series was brought well and truly alive.

Ian Botham

Back in the dressing room after play that day, I sat down in between my two team-mates and counted up the tally. Three men, five balls, no runs!

'Boys,' I said. 'We are never sitting together again.'

One of the secrets to England's success in recent years has been their attention to detail. They've left no stone unturned in finding the best people to do the best jobs, and that includes the backroom staff as well as the guys out in the middle. One of those men, David Saker, might not have been that well known outside of his native Australia, but England fans owe him a debt. As a bustling fast bowler for Victoria and Tasmania, David was as competitive a player as you will meet. If you speak to him, his love and passion for the game come through in every word he utters, and that was the case when he played, too. He also happens to be the owner of the most dangerous ball in cricket. Type that phrase into Google and see the YouTube video that appears. You'll understand why England's bowlers do what he says, lest he bowl at them in the nets!

DAVID SAKER – EVEN HEROES HAVE HEROES

During my career I've played with and against some great cricketers, and I've played on some of the world's most magnificent grounds, but like most former players the great thing about being a professional cricketer is the camaraderie you have with your team-mates. My days as a fast bowler for Victoria and then Tasmania were full of happy times on and off the field, but what I remember most are the people I met along the way. None more so than Les Stillman, the legendary coach of Victoria, who had an unbelievable passion for the game and got that across to his players in his own way. Sometimes with more success than others.

Les has a raspy thick Aussie accent and he also has a lisp, so certain phrases were best avoided if he wanted to prevent the team from bursting into laughter. Once, before a big game for Victoria, the 1995 one-day final against South Australia at the MCG, Les gathered us all together in the dressing room and gave us his pre-match talk. We had a good team and would often make it to finals or semi-finals, but we struggled to go one further and win the trophy. That was the hurdle we had to clear and Les came up with his own take on it.

'Fellath! You are a fantathtic bunch of blokth and a cracking cricket team, but there is only one thing thtanding between you and suctheth out there. A fire-breathing dragon!!'

None of us knew what he was talking about but we went along with it anyway and waited for his big finish. He went on for a while about how difficult it would be to get past this dragon and how we had to rise to the challenge. And then he raised his voice a notch.

'You will get pathd the dragon today, though, boys, and do you know why? Because a fire-breathing dragon doesn't EXISST-THTTT!!!'

We fell about laughing and went out to play, and it must have worked because we went on to win our first one-day trophy for 15 years that day, and there was no fire to be seen.

The guys I played with over the years were a rich and varied bunch, from cricketing superstars like Shane Warne to normal hard-working pros like me, and as in any workplace some were more mad than others. One such player was Peter Smith, a pace bowler who used to get so worked up about things that he would often find himself in hot water when the red mist descended. He was a fiery fast bowler who loved getting people out and, if that failed, then a bruise or too would also do. One year we were playing together for Victoria's second team and we were up against Australian Capital Territory, who had signed one of the finest cricketers ever to play the game – Gordon Greenidge. Those of us who were employed to bowl at the West Indian legend knew we would be in for a tough day, but we also knew that if we got him out we would have done something special and it would be a wicket to treasure.

I was in half-decent rhythm, so fancied my chances of getting a memorable wicket to tell my kids about, but it never happened. We should have got rid of him when he'd made about 20, but Warren Ayres, fielding at slip, put the catch down and that proved to be a big mistake, although Warren didn't quite see it that way. There are cricketers who just love playing and there are those who love everything about the game. Warren is one of the latter, because when I asked him about the drop a couple of overs later he confessed to me, 'I'm sorry I dropped the catch, of course I am, but I'm also glad because I really want to watch him bat!'

Most professional cricketers are of a similar ability, but in each team there are one or two special players, the ones their fellow pros admire, and Gordon was one of those. I'm not sure how much we meant to be in awe of him, but that day the Victorian cricketers got a lesson from an all-time great, and at one stage I thought it had all got too much for Peter Smith.

I was fielding at mid-off and he had been busting a gut all day to get Greenidge out. Even when he thought he had him plumb LBW, the appeal was somehow knocked back. He was getting more and more upset. So when he turned to me and said, 'Hey, Sakes, watch this one,' my immediate thought was that he was going to run through the crease and bowl a bouncer or, even worse, bowl a beamer and do some damage. He ran up, bowled a short ball outside off stump and Greenidge smashed it to the cover point boundary with the crack of a shotgun. I was confused. What was I supposed to be watching?

Peter came back to his mark with a big grin and said: 'How HARD does he hit it!' Even the toughest players have their heroes.

DODGY GUTS

There is something about cricket that seems to lend itself to, shall we say, the unexpected emptying of the stomach cavity. I can't think of any other sport in which the competitors either throw up or crap themselves as much as they do in cricket. Think of Dean Jones or David 'Syd' Lawrence hurling all over the pitch mid-game. I certainly suffered a few times, but luckily not out in the middle. I can remember being bent over double in Lahore, throwing up in the sink, while Mike Hendrick was next to me, bent over double, throwing up in the bath. It was not a pretty sight but, as they say, better out than in.

Perhaps it is due to the nature of the climate players play in. Obviously, it can get pretty hot and guys can become dehydrated, which is a big cause of many problems, but that has become a lot rarer these days thanks to better knowledge about replacing fluids. Perhaps it is down to the fact that cricket is played around mealtimes and there is always the chance of putting away something that disagrees with you, although again that is rarer since all the food prepared at grounds now is put under the microscope.

What you can't legislate for is a dodgy prawn the night before, which can strike you anywhere and at any time – just ask spin duo Tim May and Ashley Giles, who both came a cropper in Pakistan.

Gilo was in Faisalabad in 2005 on England Test duty following the remarkable Ashes summer, and the night before the second Test match he and a few others went to a Thai restaurant for dinner. I'm told that he had nothing more sinister than the Thai green curry, which is a pretty standard dish that shouldn't cause too much upset. He scoffed the meal, followed it up with a fresh lime soda and all was well with the world. That is, until the morning of the match when he woke up with a decidedly iffy feel to his stomach. Gilo is not one to go down easily and, since the world hadn't yet fallen out of his backside, he thought he could get through the day at least. And, besides, no one ever wants to miss a Test match.

Having lost the first Test in Multan so narrowly, by 22 runs, England were determined to hit back and the last thing they needed was their first-choice spinner pulling out on the morning of the game. Praying for Michael Vaughan to win the toss and bat, the gods didn't look down too kindly on poor Ash, and Inzamam-ul-Haq instead got to put his pads on.

The game got underway and for the first hour or so there was no real issue for the team or Gilo. He was fielding in about a fourth-slip position, trying to cover as much space as possible, when Steve Harmison bowled one that Mohammad Yousuf hit firmly into the ground and in Gilo's direction. It bounced up into his hands and, as he prefers the Aussie method of catching, with fingers pointing skywards, he had to crouch down to take it. The sudden movement downwards was just what his bowels were looking for, as he lost all control and suffered a messy accident. I remember speaking to Gilo about it and he told me that it happened so fast that it took a moment for him to actually realise what had happened. In that moment of clarity, he simply tossed the ball to another fielder and ran off. None of his teammates knew why he was off. A couple thought he had broken a finger or something, but up in the commentary box the wise old bird that is David Gower spotted it immediately, and from the back said simply. 'That is the waddle of a man who has sh*t himself.'

As a quick aside, there was also a little mishap from another former England cricketer in Sri Lanka, but this time off the field. Poor old Jonathan Agnew had the misfortune to ruin his shorts during a stint on *Test Match Special* in Galle in 2003. Now, of course, it doesn't really matter what you wear to broadcast on the radio, but I'm sure his position as the housewives-of-the-shire's favourite won't be diminished when they know he then called the rest of the day's play wearing nothing but a towel down below. With an open-air commentary position, it was a good thing it was Galle in the summer and not Headingley in the spring.

Back to Pakistan, and Tim May might recently have been the head of the Federation of International Cricketers' Associations (FICA), but in the early 1990s he was one half of a tremendous spin partnership with Shane Warne, and on the subcontinent they were the men charged with taking Australia to glory. During a one-day game in 1994 in Pakistan there was an incident that has become folklore in Australian cricket circles.

Tim had been struggling a little bit with a tender tummy throughout that trip, but it wasn't enough to keep him off the park. It was a triangular tournament, with South Africa the other team, and during one match at Rawalpindi, Tim had a moment to forget. Midway through his spell, he went up for a loud LBW appeal against Saeed Anwar, but was turned down by the umpire. Just before the umpire said not out, though, there was a sharp change in Tim's facial expression. The wicket-keeper Ian Healey and Mark Waugh at slip thought he was simply disappointed with the umpire's decision. If only.

A few overs later, May got a wicket as Michael Bevan took the catch to get rid of Aamir Sohail. Cue smiles and high fives all round, only as they all reached the huddle there was a whiff of something not quite right.

'Christ, who or what is that?' said a few of the team.

And Maysie chirps up and says, 'Sorry, boys, I appealed a bit too strongly a few overs ago and I sh*t myself. But it's all okay because it has dried up now.'

As you can imagine, he was told in no uncertain terms to get off the field and go and clean himself up. Freshly showered, he returned and got back on with the business of bowling, but I'm told that for a good few games afterwards every time he appealed it was followed up with the question: 'Need a shower, champ?' Possibly the first time an Aussie team have collectively sledged their own man, game after game.

Chris Schofield is one of the game's battlers, which is not some-thing you would necessarily associate with a spinner. He could turn his leg-break as much as the next man, but he was fast-tracked into the England team too quickly at the age of 22 and the two Tests he played were his only caps. He was almost lost to the professional game completely after being released by Lancashire, but his love of the sport meant he was prepared to keep playing minor counties cricket until Surrey gave him a shot, and his just reward was a brilliant couple of seasons for them which culmi-nated in an England recall for Twenty20 cricket. He had battled back from oblivion to wear the three lions again, and that sets him apart as a player of real substance.

CHRIS SCHOFIELD –
BETTER THAN AVERAGE

B eing a professional cricketer can be a fragile existence – one minute you're on top of the world and the next you're nowhere. But, throughout it all, a love of the game keeps you going and certainly in my case I wouldn't have kept on going and trying to make it as a professional if I didn't love it so much. Along the way you are given support by those close to you, whether it is your parents or your friends or your coaches, and when you're feeling a bit low they can help pick you up and get you ready for the next challenge. Rarely, if ever, do they knock you down – that is the job of the opposition.

So imagine my surprise and dismay when a man who was supposed to back me all the way actually gave me a huge crisis of confidence. I had been making strides at Lancashire, bowling well and taking wickets in the second XI, when I received a letter inviting me to play for a young England side in an Under-19 tournament in the Southwest. It would involve teams from what you would now call associate nations, sides like Ireland U19s and Denmark U19s, and naturally England would expect to win. The letter was handwritten by none other than Mickey Stewart, the former England coach, Surrey legend and father of Alec.

It was a very proud day for me, but as I read through the letter carefully a second time, my pride turned to bewilderment and, if I'm honest, anger. He wrote: 'Congratulations on your selection to the squad. We are delighted to have you join our group of players . . .' and so on. Then the part I will never forget. 'This is a tournament where England are allowed to field two average players along with the rest of the squad, so in case you're wondering why we've picked you, it is because you and Robert Key are our two average players.'

Well, that wasn't on really, was it? I showed the letter to my mum and dad and they were just as upset about it as me. How could you pick a young lad to play for England at any level and then go and tell him that he's an average player? I had to know why Mickey had been so harsh, when I thought I deserved to be there just like any other player, and certainly Robert Key was better than average.

It festered away for a while, leaving me with a few doubts before I turned up to meet the squad on the first day. When I got there, Mickey was all smiles, as if he had never said or written a cross word in his life. Before I could quiz him about what he'd written, he said: 'Hello, Chris, great to see you. I'm expecting good things from you – after all, you and Robert are our two over-age players for the tournament.'

Eh?!

It was an Under-19 tournament, but because England were playing against the associate teams they had entered an Under-17 team instead and were allowed to pick two 'over-age' players. Suddenly everything made sense, and that first England call-up remains a special one.

A year later, I made my first-class debut for Lancashire and enjoyed another seven years as a professional at Old Trafford. In that time I was lucky to play with some of the greats of the game, the likes of Mike Atherton, Wasim Akram, Glen Chapple and Freddie Flintoff. And, as with every dressing room, there was great banter and some very funny moments, none more so than when we were playing a game against Kent at Old Trafford on a rare sunny day and Fred was going great guns with the bat. Unfortunately, he was struck amidships by Dean Headley and had to take refuge back in the pavilion. There are many ways of dealing with what you might call 'sore plums' but nothing beats a soothing bowl of cold water. As there were no bowls to hand, Fred had to make do with a pint glass of water and ice. So, there he was, cooling himself for about half an hour or so. Not long after he'd finished, Gary Yates, our off spinner, came into the dressing room. He'd just finished batting himself and declared, 'It's bloody roasting out there, I'm gasping!' Well, in those days you didn't have the ready supply of isotonic drinks that you do now, so someone pointed out to him that there was a pint of iced water waiting for him on the side. Right next to where Freddie Flintoff changed.

He might have been small by name and small for a fast bowler, but Gladstone Small had a giant heart and was as quality a seam bowler as you are ever likely to find. He also became a big character on my favourite tour of them all, to Australia in 1986/87, in which he took the final catch that secured us the Ashes on Aussie soil. His performance in Melbourne that won us those Ashes was Boy's Own stuff. Drafted into the side to replace Graham Dilley at the last minute, he grabbed his chance with both hands and delivered a man-of-the-match display of swing bowling. It was a high point that we celebrated together in classic style. It might have been his first England tour but he was the perfect tourist and great company at the dinner table. Something he retains to this day. And as part of the all-conquering Warwickshire side of the 1990s, it could be forgotten that he and Tim Munton were the rocks on which that team was built. Gladdy was the epitome of the professional cricketer. Hard and uncompromising on the field, and a lovely man to spend time with off it.

GLADSTONE SMALL – DRESSING-ROOM HIERARCHY

Walking into the England dressing room for your first Test match brings about feelings of excitement, awe and a touch of nervousness. But, above all, is your desire to do well and show everyone that you deserve to be there. It is something you work so hard for that when you finally get the chance, you don't want anyone to take it away.

I think that is why some players, certainly in my day, could be a little timid when they first played for England, because there were such big characters and big names from the game in that dressing room with you. Nowadays, the players have spent much more time going through the ECB's academies and such like that they know a few faces right from the off. What hasn't changed, though, is the pecking order in the dressing room. The captain at the top, the senior pros just under that, the established players next and the young rookies right at the bottom. It is all part and parcel of the game and everyone goes through it, no matter whether you are Kevin Pietersen, Shane Warne or even Sir Viv Richards.

Having made my debut in the summer of 1986 I was very excited to be picked for the Ashes tour that winter and, although we'd been tagged as the team that couldn't bat, couldn't bowl and couldn't field, I thought we had a chance to do something special, and so it proved. I was one of the new boys on that trip and was determined to make the most of it. Australia is a fantastic place where you can't fail to have a good time, so when we arrived in Brisbane, the venue for the first Test, 10 days before the match in order to acclimatise, I thought I could get used to it.

When the first Test arrived, I missed out on selection and was 12th man for the game.

Like all good 12th men, I made sure that the guys who were in the team had everything they needed to get their jobs done. One of the most important things was to get the drinks ready because it was ferociously hot out there and the boys needed to take on fluids throughout the day. We had a few tour sponsors for that trip and one of them was Gatorade, the energy drinks company. In those days, it meant a giant green drinks bottle for each player and a massive box of Gatorade powder which you mixed with water to get the desired drink. Each player liked to have his drink mixed differently, some quite strong, others with the minimum of powder, and it was my job to get their orders just right.

It was after the close of play on day one that Ian Botham pulled me to one side to have a chat. We were 198 for two; Beefy was due to go in at the fall of two more wickets. There had been no need to put in his drinks order before now, but the following day he was sure to bat so he wanted a word.

'Now listen here, youngster,' he said. 'You're in charge of my drinks in this game and that is a very important responsibility because I'm going to be gasping in this heat.'

'No problem, Beefy, just tell me how you like it and I'll get the Gatorade mixed up.'

'Gatorade?! I'm not interested in any bloody Gatorade. I want you to pour two cans of lager into that green bottle and then top it up with lemonade, got that?'

'Oh, right, but where am I going to get the lager from?' I asked.

'Tour sponsor, of course!'

Just as Gatorade were one of our sponsors, so too were Castle-maine XXXX and they always left plenty of produce for the end-of-day wind-down. I had to squirrel some away for mid-match performance. The next day Beefy went out to bat and got stuck into the Aussies in the way that only he could. He smashed Merv Hughes all over the Gabba in a display of hitting reminiscent of his 1981 heroics. He batted for just over four hours and throughout that knock I took him a few drinks.

By the third delivery of his 'mixture' he told me I needed to make a minor alteration. 'Reduce the lemonade content, youngster, I'm getting a bit bloated.' I did as he asked, and 138 runs later he had put England in control of the game.

Getting to play alongside legends of the game like that was always a thrill, and it was the same when I played for Warwickshire and with Brian Lara. It was the 1994 season and he was coming over on the back of his world record 375 scored against England that winter. He arrived in Birmingham and set the place on fire. He was just incredible, scoring more runs than we knew what to do with, culminating in another world record 501 in first-class cricket.

By then I was a senior pro at the club and that brought its own perks, the main one being that of the three beds in the physio's room, one was called simply 'Gladdy's bed', because if I wasn't bowling I could be found laid out on it having a kip as the physios went to work on the other two. No one really minded or bothered me; it was my resting spot and I had earned it.

When Brian arrived, my sleep patterns were thrown into jeopardy for two reasons. The first was that, whenever Brian went out to bat, you watched. There was no time for sleeping when he was at the crease because he was just incredible. The second reason was that Brian was a bit of a night owl himself and, after burning the candle at both ends – usually with his great mate Dwight Yorke, who was playing for Aston Villa at the time – he would be looking for a place to kip. And, in this case, the star overseas player trumped the reliable club stalwart, especially when he announced himself with 147 and 106 in his first two championship matches.

Where he really got me, though, was not by nicking my bed in the first place, but by bringing his own duvet into the dressing room with him. He was a warm-blooded Caribbean man so Edgbaston in May was a chilly experience for him. But the moment I saw it, all I could think was, Why didn't I bring a duvet?

I couldn't be too upset with him because he more than made up for it on the field. What happened the day after he scored his 501 really summed him up. Not only had he been in huge demand on the day by every media outlet you can think of to talk about his record-breaking feat, but he'd naturally wanted to celebrate the achievement, which he duly did. The next day, however, was a Benson and Hedges Cup semi-final against Surrey at The Oval, so he was back on duty. But, boy, did he need a kip.

He rocked up to the ground and, as we were in the field, he suggested going down to fine leg so he could run around a bit and get some life into his legs. That didn't work. He then came up into the slips and realised he was struggling to see the ball. He asked if he could go off to try and get himself right. He promptly fell asleep in the dressing room and remained in his slumber until it came for us to bat. He was our No. 3 and match-winner, so I thought it was time for him to get up as Dominic Ostler and Michael Burns went out to open, but our coach, Bob Woolmer, told me to leave him alone and find my own place to sleep! We lost a couple of wickets and he was still sleeping. We lost a third and he was still sleeping. Chasing 268 to win, we really needed our star man, so eventually Bob said to wake him up. He got up, rubbed his eyes, put his kit on, strapped on his pads and the moment he was finished another wicket fell and in he went. He scored 70 magical runs and won us the game.

It was like watching a fairy tale all summer long. On that basis, I was happy for him to be our very own Goldilocks sleeping in the bear's bed.

It takes all sorts to make up a dressing room, and it takes all sorts to be a professional cricketer. Some think about the game and what goes into it rather deeply, and others just go out there and let their instincts run wild. It is fair to say that I was in the latter category and Jeremy Snape was in the former. As an off spinner who could bat a bit, Jeremy Snape was a proven county cricketer who managed to make the leap to the England team in one-day cricket, where he could use his theories and ideas to maximum effect. As a spinner, your ability to con the batsman is a must and 'Snapper' had that. He was always trying to squeeze something out of a situation and it was that attention to detail that helped Leicestershire accomplish so much during a golden period in the 1990s. His return to the England Twenty20 set-up in 2007 was a testament to his longevity and his constant evolution as a cricketer, and it came as no surprise to me when he moved into the psychology of sport and became a valuable asset to the South African cricket team as part of their backroom staff.

JEREMY SNAPE – GETTING THE BLOOD PUMPING

Finding out what makes sportsmen, especially cricketers, tick has become an area of huge interest to me since I stopped playing, but it was always there even in my playing days.

I didn't analyse my team-mates too rigorously but as a spin bowler, when you're trying to get a batsman out, there is an element of trying to work him out mentally before actually doing it on the pitch. You try to play on his weaknesses, or his perceived weaknesses, and you try to force him to do things that he otherwise wouldn't want to do. Sometimes, you just get him out.

I always endeavoured to take my cricket reasonably seriously, but given the number of people involved in a team environment and how much time cricketers spend with each other, you can't be serious all the time. And at Leicestershire we had a few characters who would lighten the mood and keep spirits up, even when things weren't going that well.

One such player was Paul Nixon, who is literally as mad as a badger. But if he's on your side, the hours of entertainment he can provide are priceless. 'Nico' was a livewire behind the stumps, full of energy, never stopped talking and cajoling and encouraging other players; but when you talk as much as he does, inevitably a lot of it becomes just noise and that is what got under the skin of opposition batsmen. They never understood just how he could keep going morning, noon and night. Several players would get out just to stop listening to him, and I think he knew that!

However, one player who found a way to shut him out was Murray Goodwin, playing for Sussex back in 2003 during the final County Championship match of the season down at Hove. It was a game Sussex won easily during their period of county dominance, thanks to big runs from Murray and a ton from Chris Adams. I remember it being at the end of a long season for us at Leicestershire and, as a result, a few of the lads let their hair down once it became clear where the game was headed. We decided to have a bit of fun and, in David Masters's case, it actually paid off when he continued his knock as the nightwatchman on day three after a heavy night and proceeded to hit the most brilliant hundred you've ever seen despite being absolutely trollied. He had to be woken up just before play to make it out to the middle, but once he was there he played Mushtaq Ahmed as if he were a net bowler. It was great stuff, but that wasn't even the funniest event of that game.

It was midway through the final session on the second day and Murray was on about 300 and batting like a dream. We were struggling to get anything going and things were just a bit flat in the field. Even Nico wasn't his usual busy self. We needed something to perk us up and it just so happened that there was this new drug on the market called Viagra.

For those who've been living in a cave for the last 20 years, it helps men who have trouble getting or sustaining an erection. One of our players, who shall remain nameless, had access to a few of these pills and thought it might be an idea to crush them up and add them to Nico's energy drink at the break. He duly sank the lot and went back to fielding behind the stumps.

Despite being well off the pace of the game, we went for four slips and a gully during the remainder of the day, with each of us doing our best to talk about sex, porn magazines and the beautiful women we'd seen recently. Nico was completely and utterly oblivious to the direction the conversation consistently went in, joining in occasionally but nothing more. The rest of us were in stitches throughout the session, turning the chat back to sex at every opportunity, while looking to see what effect it was having on Nico.

He certainly appeared to be enjoying the cricket he was playing that evening and he was still enjoying it by the time we got to the dressing room after play. We had also sent the 12th man out to pick up a porn magazine during the session and got him to cut out the photos and stick them all around Nico's changing area. He had naked women on the walls, inside his bag, and even inside his shoes. Yet at no stage did he even acknowledge it, or comment on it. He just thought the lads were being a bit childish. We were, but for different reasons.

The following morning, the lads were still in stitches over the prank and it was time to come clean, but not before Nico pulled the team doctor over to one side to confess the lengthy period of arousal he had just experienced. Apparently he'd had trouble sleeping, and each time he tried to find a new position to lie in, he couldn't roll over.

Alec Stewart became England's most-capped cricketer for two reasons. He was a bloody good player and he never settled for anything less than the very best from himself. If ever a man wrung every last drop out of his ability and career it was Stewie, and he has a fabulous career to look back on. From the moment I first met him and played with him until he called stumps in 2003, he left no stone unturned in the search for excellence. At a time when English cricket went through a bit of a rough patch and picked more players than we ever knew played the game professionally, Stewie was a reassuring constant and gave everything he had for the cause. He's as polite and gentlemanly as they come, always immaculately turned out, but he was as tough as old boots, too. A spell Down Under in Aussie club cricket made sure of that, and he never took a backwards step. A genuine British bulldog, who made sure everything was neat and tidy when he left.

ALEC STEWART – ANGER MANAGEMENT

In over 20 years as a professional cricketer I've been in some interesting dressing rooms, full of characters, jokers and quick-witted one-liners. And most of the banter that goes on keeps you chuckling during those long periods either in the field or in the dressing room when someone else is piling on the runs. Fair play to Beefy for trying to collect a few of these stories for posterity, but if I'm honest most of the tales are either too X-rated for public consumption or immediately forgettable.

There are always one or two exceptions and during my playing days there were a couple of incidents that stood out and had me in stitches for two completely different reasons. The first was funny because it was supposed to be funny.

It was a fantastic championship game back in 1988 against Lancashire in Southport and, despite being on the end of a Wasim Akram hat-trick in the first innings, Surrey were in a position to make the running for a win. We set them 272 to win in 70 overs and they got up to 271 for nine at the close. It was a terrific game of cricket that neither side deserved to lose. It didn't look like being that close at tea, though, when Lancs were five down and with over 120 runs still needed. At that stage, with Wasim and Neil Fairbrother at the crease, it looked like a draw might be their best chance and they were certainly aiming not to lose any more wickets before the break.

It was the last over before tea and Wasim was facing, so our captain, Ian Greig, decided to bring on our spinner, Keith Medlycott, for an over. I was keeping; we had a slip and a gully as well as David Ward at short leg. Wasim was full of concentration, trying not to get out, at which point Wardy whipped out a bright red clown's nose from his pocket and shoved it on the end of his conk. Poor old Was broke down in giggles as Wardy just stood there, stony-faced – apart from the red nose, of course – and waited for each ball to be bowled.

Wasim could hardly see the ball for the water in his eyes, he was laughing so hard.

He managed to get through the over, Wardy took off the red nose, popped it back in his pocket and Wasim gave him a huge hug as they walked off for tea. I'm not sure what would have happened had he got out in that over, but it just goes to show some people will do anything to get a wicket.

That was a light-hearted moment for all of us, but dressing rooms are not always that happy. A few years later, we were playing at Colchester and I witnessed one of the biggest fits of rage that I have ever seen from a cricketer, and these days it would have come with an ECB disciplinary penalty.

A few of us were watching the game from the changing room, which is a long way from the middle at Colchester and you have to stand on the benches to peer through the window to see what is going on. As we were perched on this bench Graham Thorpe got out cheaply and was on his way back to the dressing room. We looked at each other in the way that says, 'Shall we get out of here to let him stew in peace?' We thought it would be okay because Thorpey wasn't Mark Ramprakash and he wouldn't throw a wobbly. By now we could hear his studs clicking on the floor and it would be obvious if we made a dash for it, so we stayed put. The door was shut and it was one of those older wooden doors that needed a bit of encouragement to open.

Thorpey wasn't in the mood to encourage anything and he tried to force it open. BANG!! His foot connected with the door and not only did it open but his foot and half his still-padded-up leg went through it, leaving him stuck on one leg in the doorway. Now, those of you who have been in dressing rooms before will know that in the immediate aftermath of getting out cheaply, the batsman doesn't want anyone to talk to him, touch him or even look at him as he gets the dismissal out of his system, and this was no different. Thorpey might have had his foot through a door but no one was going to get involved.

He pulled his leg and the pad was stuck; he pushed the door and his leg was stuck; he grunted and groaned and huffed and puffed and nothing moved anywhere. The three of us in the room didn't know where to look, except into our shirts where we tried to stifle our sniggers.

After a good few minutes of cursing and energetic pulling, Thorpey gave up and said softly, almost pathetically, 'Lads, can you get me out of the door, please?' That was it, we all burst into laughter and even Thorpey saw the funny side. It was less funny when he had to pay for the damage, but at least he was over his dismissal.

I saw red a few times, too. None more so than in 2000 when playing for Surrey at the end of a season in which I had done pretty well for England. I had been in the runs and the team had had some success, so I was feeling pretty good about things, but then I went back to the club I love and lost it. I'd got out early for not very many, and on the way back to the dressing rooms at The Oval you have to climb a lot of steps to get there through the members. I was a bit annoyed at getting out and overheard one member say to another: 'Bloody typical of Stewart, he only really tries for England.'

That was like a red rag to a bull and, I'll admit, I was going to grab that member by the throat and have it out with him à la Cantona. I turned to confront him at the precise moment my studs got caught in the ground and I fell flat on my face, with my kit sprawling everywhere. I was so embarrassed. I quickly grabbed my gloves, bat and helmet and went on my way without lamping anyone!

RISE AND SHINE

There are all sorts of pranks that get played in the dressing-room, most of which are pretty harmless. I used to get up to my fair share, whether it was setting fire to a newspaper some-one was reading or squeezing toothpaste in their shoes. Mostly, it was the result of boredom and the desire to liven things up a bit. I never put a great deal of thought into my wind-ups, but when players take the time to set up their pranks properly the outcome can be well worthwhile.

Back in 1998 David 'Bumble' Lloyd picked a young Andrew Flintoff to play for England. He knew he was a special player, but perhaps, at 20, he wasn't quite ready. He returned to Lanca-shire after an indifferent start, but soon came back and went on to become one of England's finest all-rounders.

Along for most of that ride was his best mate, Steve Harmi-son, who would terrify batsmen around the world with his height and pace. Together they were a fearsome duo with the ball in hand, and off the field they were as thick as thieves. The two would often have interconnecting rooms in hotels so that they could play darts and keep each other company.

During a tour to Pakistan in 2006 Fred's old coach Bumble, who was now working as a pundit for Sky Sports, was explaining to the pair of them that he was having a terrible time sleeping. His room at the hotel was facing a local mosque and, when the call to prayer went out at about five in the morning, he would be woken up and couldn't get back to sleep. For those who haven't experienced it, the call to prayer involves a man chanting a few phrases in quite a loud voice and you don't sleep through it.

Ever the sympathetic souls, Fred and Harmy listened to Bumble's woes and carried on training. Once practice had finished, they both ventured into town to see what goodies they might be able to get hold of. And on their travels they spotted an alarm clock in the shape of a mosque. The shop owner was delighted to play for them the call to prayer it sounded and that was enough, they bought it.

That evening they snuck into Bumble's room in the hotel and planted the alarm clock. At 2 a.m., a happily snoozing David Lloyd was given a rude awakening. Thinking it was the mosque outside, he waited for it to stop; but when it didn't, and seemed to be a bit louder, he went ballistic. Hunting it down, he pulled out clothes, drawers, irons and ironing boards, all sorts, trying to find it. And when he eventually got hold of it he couldn't work out how to turn it off. In the end, the removal of the batteries and a hurl across the floor did the trick.

Flustered and more than a little irritated, he eventually got back into bed and fell fast asleep. At 3 a.m. he discovered the cheeky pair had invested twice the money, as the second alarm went off! Poor old Bumble, he didn't know what to do with himself. He can be a bit eccentric at times, but when he hasn't had a good night's kip he ventures into the territory of just plain mad, and we certainly felt the effects in the commentary box on that trip.

Bumble knew it was fair game, though, and is not too shy of pulling a prank or two himself. In Sri Lanka in 2007 he managed to catch one of the current crop with a beauty. The teams and the media were moving from Colombo to Galle for the next match of the tour and, if you read the local paper, you would know that there was a lot of talk about the new Southern Expressway, which they were building to connect the west coast to the south of the island. It was still under construction so not yet open, but the excitement was mounting because it would reduce the time it took to cover the 116 kilometres between the two towns from six hours to two. In fact, on the most recent trip to Sri Lanka, in 2012, the team bus used the expressway and flew down to Galle in no time at all.

That was more to some players' liking, but back in 2007 there were a few grumbles about the hardship of sitting on a bus for several hours. Bumble knew they would be feeling the effects of a six- or seven-hour bus journey, so he planted the perfect set-up with the England team manager, Phil Neale, who was in charge of all the logistics and transport. On arriving in Galle, Bumble deliberately 'accidentally' bumped into Kevin Pietersen at an England training session and asked about the journey down from Colombo.

'Jeez, Bumble, it was terrible! Six hours on a bloody bus – my back is killing me. I don't know why we didn't fly,' said Kevin.

'Oh, really? Six hours?! Why didn't you take the expressway? It only took us an hour and three-quarters, we just ate up the empty road,' said Bumble, with a straight face.

'What are you talking about?'

'There's this new motorway that they've built, but nobody uses it because it's a toll road. Thankfully, Sky Sports got us on it and we whizzed down.'

Cue much effing and blinding from Kevin, demanding to know why they hadn't used this 'magical' road. This is where

Bumble is a master. There is no one better at telling a porky than him, and somehow he keeps the straightest of faces, so you would believe even the most outrageous lie. This was easy for him.

And with that Kevin went straight to Phil to ask him why the driver wouldn't take the motorway. 'I'm afraid the ECB wouldn't pay the toll fare, Kevin. You know how tight things can be, they just didn't see the need to stump up more cash for the trip.'

'That is ridiculous,' snarled Kevin. 'How much was it?'

Now, this is where you have to give Phil his due. He, too, somehow managed to keep a straight face as he told Kevin the figure. Bear in mind that the exchange rate of pounds sterling to Sri Lankan rupee was about one to 130.

'It was two thousand six hundred, Kev.'

'Well, that's not a massive amount of money – surely they could have stretched to two thousand six hundred pounds for the players?'

'Oh, not pounds, Kev. Two thousand six hundred rupees.'

At which point Kevin almost sank to his knees and pulled out enough money to cover the toll and more. Bumble had got his man and promptly set his sights on his next victim.

I've long said that my favourite tour as a player was the 1986/87 tour of Australia because we won the Ashes Down Under when no one gave us a prayer. It is the toughest tour of the lot for an Englishman, as well as being the most fun, but not even I thought that it would take 24 years for another side to go there and complete the feat. When they did, they accomplished it in wonderful style, winning 3–1 and all matches by an innings. That is a thumping, and without question much of the credit for such a success must be laid at the feet of Andrew Strauss. He was a magnificent captain of England and that series in 2010/11 was his crowning moment. Always leading by example, he was a modern captain who understood the history and traditions of the game, and gave it and the opposition his full respect. He was statesmanlike and I must admit I felt huge pride watching him and his team go about their business. He wasn't just a captain, though – he was a fine opening batsman and the only Englishman to score not one, but two tons during that famous Ashes series of 2005. And, to top it off, he's a bloody decent bloke as well. The fact that it looks likely he will stay in the game in some shape or form in the future is great news for English cricket, because if he is anything like the asset he was on the field, the game will be in great hands.

ANDREW STRAUSS –
SOMEONE CALL SECURITY

The greatest test of any international cricket team is the ability to win matches and series away from home. That is where you really earn your stripes. That's not to say that winning at home is easy, it still takes a lot of hard work and effort to win any game of cricket, but at home you've got most things in your favour. The conditions that you've grown up playing in, your home comforts that make you feel relaxed, the food, the weather and the familiarity of the grounds all add up to give the home side an advantage.

The key is how to get over that hurdle on tour. One of the big features of my time in the England dressing room has been letting the team enjoy and embrace the places we visit. You generally find that the more you immerse yourself in the local environment and take time with the people you meet, the more likely you are to succeed – if, of course, you've looked after everything you can cricket-wise.

It was the mindset we used in Australia in 2010/11 and it is clearly how Alastair Cook and the current squad approached their successful trip to India in 2012, which is one of the toughest assignments in the game. During my time, the best we managed in India was the 1–1 draw in 2006, perhaps most famous for the 'Ring of Fire' Test in Mumbai, which we won to square the series with the strains of Johnny Cash ringing in our ears thanks to Andrew Flintoff's rustic taste in music.

Following the Test series we embarked on a seven-match one-day series that finished up in Indore. We had fully embraced the Indian culture and were enjoying the trip, but our 5–1 reverse goes to show that loving the country you're touring will only get you so far if your cricket is not up to scratch. Still, it was fascinating to see how this country was evolving into the economic powerhouse and growing super-power it has become. With such development come things like more high-quality hotels and restaurants, and some cities in India are leading the way.

However, back in 2006 the smaller cities didn't really have a wide choice of eateries. So, after two and a half months on tour, during which we had taken the local cuisine to our hearts, we were desperate for something different from a chicken tikka dish or a dal makhani. It so happened that one of the lads had heard of a newly installed Pizza Hut in Indore and was keen to try it out. Despite what Shane Warne or Beefy Botham will tell you, pizza is not the normal evening meal for today's elite crick-eters, but a little of what you fancy every now and again does you good, so with that in mind we decided to have a team dinner at the local Pizza Hut. When we walked through the door, the manager of the restaurant had to rub his eyes at the sight of the likes of Kevin Pietersen and Andrew Flintoff coming to eat at his franchise. He wasn't exactly used to this kind of clientèle, but he found us his best table and sat about 16 of us down to eat along the window of the restaurant.

It was a pretty fun evening and we all certainly enjoyed tuck-ing into our Stuffed Crust Meat Feasts, but after about 10 minutes or so one of the guys looked round and there was a crowd of about 20 or 30 people standing by the window, watching us eat. The spectacle of the entire England team having a bite could be considered a bit of a curiosity, and if you happened to be walking by you might look and point and then move on. At least that is what might happen in most places – not India. Cricket is a religion in India.

By the time we'd finished our meal there were no fewer than 2,000 people jostling for position to watch us eat. Playing a cover drive in front of 90,000 at the MCG is something I thrived on and relished; making sure I chewed my pizza properly because I had 2,000 watching every mouthful was not something I ever thought I'd have to do. And that is why winning cricket matches in India is not just about what you do on the field, but how you cope with life off it.

Thankfully, we had our security man, Reg Dickason, out with us, plus a couple of other Indian security men, because this sort of thing was not uncommon. We were all ushered into our waiting coach, smiling for a few photos and signing a few autographs on the way, and everyone went home happy – reporting on the exquisite table manners of the England team.

When it comes to security, though, things are not always that straightforward and, as easy a ride as Reg normally has, every now and again he is called into action. Reg has become a fixture with the England side over the past eight years or so, and he's easy to spot with his big bushy moustache twirling in the afternoon sun. A burly former policeman from Australia, Reg is our security expert and he has had a major role to play at times, such as in the decision about whether to return to India following the Mumbai terror attacks in 2008. However, the truth is most of the time he hardly breaks into a sweat unless he's by the pool.

On the one occasion when he needed to leap into action, though, he did just that and proved that his instincts remain as sharp as that of an opening batsman. A group of us were enjoying a few drinks in our Sydney hotel bar late into the night following the end of the Australian tour in 2006/07. We had just won the one-day triangular series and, after a tough Ashes series, it was a chance to unwind. At around 3 a.m. there was a huge smash in the hotel lobby, which took us all by surprise. Whereas the players shrugged their shoulders and turned back to their drinks, Reg shot out of his chair and went towards the commotion. It turned out that masked robbers had broken into the hotel and were trying to relieve people and the hotel of whatever valuables they could. This included our team physio, Dean Conway, who, for those who don't know, is a giant rugby prop from the Welsh Valleys.The request to hand over his phone and wallet is usually swatted away like a minor inconvenience on the streets of Cardiff on a Friday night. But these men weren't drunk and waddling down St Mary Street – they had knives and meant business, so Deano reluctantly handed over his belongings.

It was at this point that we wondered what Reg might do to them. This was his chance to do his best John McClane impression by beating up the bad guys and saving the day. Instead, we saw him running in the opposite direction, beckoning us to follow him. We took his advice and followed him as he ushered us towards and out of an emergency exit and simply told us to RUN! We did as we were told, although at that time of the night and after a few drinks our running more resembled waddling while the robbers tried to get access to the hotel safe and then fled themselves before the police arrived.

The bottom line is that, in the heat of the moment, Reg made sure we were safe and secure, which is ultimately what he is paid to do. But that small detail was pushed to one side afterwards, and rest assured we regularly reminded him that the act of running away was not what we expected from our Aussie 'tough guy'. Especially when the two animals on the crest emblazoned on the front of the baggy green cap are the kangaroo and the emu. Why? Because, dear Reg, they are physically unable to take a backwards step!

There is a rich history and tradition of Caribbean influence on the England cricket team, from guys like Phil DeFreitas and Gladstone Small to Mark Butcher. And to that list you can add Alex Tudor, a brilliant fast bowler at his best and one who would surely have played more international cricket had his powerful body allowed. He had pace and height, the perfect combination for a fast bowler, and watching him impress on debut against Australia in Australia made everyone sit up and take notice. I thought we might have unearthed a real gem, but sadly he couldn't quite string games together when he needed to. He was and is, though, one of the friendliest and loveliest guys in the game. Always smiling and laughing, and ready with a hand-shake and a chat whenever you see him, 'Tudes' clearly loves the game, and it is great to see him giving something back by running coaching courses for kids.

ALEX TUDOR – WOULD YOU LIKE A FLAKE WITH THAT?

Fast bowling is hard. A lot of fun but hard work. No one knows more than me just how much of a toll it takes on the body. Sprinting to the crease, taking off, turning, landing hard and letting go of that ball at high speed – the body is not designed to do that naturally and, as a result, all of us suffer. Some more than others. Still, it gives me a huge sense of pride to have achieved what I did as a bowler and, although I could bat a bit, taking wickets always gave me the biggest thrill.

Whenever I meet someone new who wants to talk to me about cricket and my England career, there are only two things they ever really want to discuss. Is it the four for 89 on debut against Australia in Perth, where I managed to bag both Waugh twins in that haul? No. Is it the five for 44 at Trent Bridge against the Aussies in 2001? No. It is being denied a Test hundred by one run and being felled by a Brett Lee bouncer.

It's a little unusual for a fast bowler to be reminded constantly of his batting, although I suspect Tino Best might know how that feels after what he did at Edgbaston during 2012.

The bouncer was not a nice moment at all, as you might imagine. I reckon Brett Lee was bowling at his absolute peak during that series in 2002. He was fast, hostile and he actually enjoyed watching the batsmen dive for cover. He did it to the tail-enders as well and I suppose, to his mind, the man holding the bat was there to be targeted. I remember he also gave Andy Caddick a torrid time. Anyway, the fact is, he got one to rear up from just short of a length and let's say it took me by surprise!

The innings against New Zealand is, thankfully, the one that comes up far more often, and I don't mind talking about it because it gives me the chance to put the record straight. It was my third Test match and my first at home, so I was experiencing a lot of new things and enjoying them. I had picked up the wicket of Stephen Fleming in the first innings, so at least I had contributed, and I felt that more would come.

With the bat in the first innings, things had gone well. I scored 32 not out in a small total of just 132, and then watched as Caddy and Alan Mullally ripped through them to bowl them out for 107 and leave us with 208 to get on a pitch that was suiting the bowlers.

There were only a few overs maximum for us to face, so Nasser Hussain, the captain and No. 3, wanted a nightwatchman. There wasn't a designated man like Jimmy Anderson back then, so he just turned to me and said, 'Right, Tudes, you got a few in the first innings, I want you to do it.' I was happy to have a go and by the close I was 0 not out, with my Surrey team-mate Mark Butcher there on 3.

The next morning, both Nasser and Graham Gooch (who had been helping me out with my batting on the side) gave great speeches to the team about the need for someone to step up and take responsibility for scoring the runs. Don't leave it to someone else, was the mantra. I took it on board and went out there.

If it was straight I defended it and if it was wide I had a go. It just so happened that when I had a go, the ball seemed to fly to the boundary. Butch was out for 33, but Nasser and I put on 98 together and broke the back of the chase. By the time he went, there were just 34 runs needed and I had moved into the 80s. People were enjoying my knock and wanted to see me get to a hundred, but I wasn't thinking about personal milestones – I just wanted us to win the game.

In truth, I thought I'd get there and, even if I didn't, I thought there would be plenty more opportunities to get a century. I wasn't to know I'd only play 10 Tests! Thorpey came out and said, 'Don't worry, Tudes. I'll get a few singles, give you the strike and get you to your hundred.'

I misjudged the mood and told him, 'Don't be silly. Let's just win the game and then worry about who's got what. We've got to win the game.'

Thorpey was such a quality player that he took them apart himself and whacked a quick-fire 21. It all meant that, while I needed five to get to my hundred, the team only needed four to win and that duly came from a top edge over the keeper's head. I didn't expect Thorpey to get booed because I'd been left stranded on 99, but he did and that was so unfair. In the days that followed everyone came up to me, saying, 'I can't believe what Thorpe did to you!'

But I have to set the record straight: Thorpey didn't do anything to me. He helped me win a Test match for England and that is worth more than one man's search for three figures. Why is 100 so much better than 99 anyway? It is only one run. I will defend him all the way on this one. I had a great time, got plenty of attention and enjoyed breaking the record for the highest score by an English nightwatchman, beating Harold Larwood's 98, set during the Bodyline series of 1932/33. That was good enough for me.

It gave Nasser his first win as England captain in his first Test match, reversing a trend going back to the early 1980s. He was a good captain for England and put a bit of toughness back into our cricket when it needed it, but sometimes he went over the top. As he did on tour in 1999 in Durban, when I went to get on the team bus.

Both Nasser and Duncan Fletcher were sticklers for good timekeeping, so you made sure you were not late. On this particular occasion, I wasn't late but as I approached the bus it started moving away. I ran and caught up with it, banged on the door and got it to stop and let me on. Nasser had been under pressure during the trip and he often used rows with people to let off steam. He completely flew off the handle at me, accusing me of being late and so on. I knew I wasn't, so we ended up having a huge argument, which really isn't like me. I was really upset at him for taking his anger out on me; it hurt and even to this day it still makes me feel uncomfortable.

Poor old Darren Maddy, though. He was batting in the net when Nasser stood as our umpire, and so I took out my own frustrations in the only way I knew. I gave Darren a torrid time, bowling fast and short to have him hopping around. He must have wondered what he'd done to deserve such a barrage.

Nasser wasn't the only player with a fierce temper. One of my best mates in the game, Mark Ramprakash, also had the ability to let rip – but, thankfully, never at me. I once saw him unleash on a poor server at KFC, though! We'd stopped off at a motorway service station on the way home from a game and he was feeling a bit tense. He got to the front of the queue, looked at the menu and said: 'Can I have a couple of pieces of chicken, some fries, a Coke and a side of coleslaw, please?'

The girl behind the counter said: 'Why don't you just have a two-piece meal, sir?'

'That's not what I asked for!' Ramps replied. 'I want a couple of pieces of chicken, some fries, a Coke and a side of coleslaw.'

'But, sir, you should get a two-piece meal,' said the girl, helpfully.

Ramps was just not having any of it. I had to step in to calm him down and explain that she was only trying to save him a bit of money. But Ramps was in a bad mood and just snapped. I love the guy and tease him about it now, but it took me by surprise.

Phil Tufnell is everybody's second favourite cricketer. His ability with a cricket ball when bowling his left-arm spin was exceptional and he produced many a magnificent performance but it was, and is, his 'cheeky chappie' persona that took him into everyone's heart. Able to produce such magic on a cricket field, he is also the lovable rogue with a twinkle in his eye. His subsequent career, thanks to programmes like A Question of Sport *and* I'm a Celebrity . . . , *has come as no surprise to those of us who know him, although I think he has surprised himself a little bit by the way it has all turned out. The one thing to remember about Tuffers is that he is a very smart man indeed. He might play the fool on camera and in the commentary box, but he is anything but. And if you listen carefully to what he has to say on the game, more often than not he is not only right, but he'll have told you something you didn't know.*

PHIL TUFNELL – TAKING AIM

During my early days with the Middlesex first team, myself and Angus Fraser used to travel along with the team, and sometimes we played and at other times we didn't. We were 12th or 13th men for the day – Gussy was a much more effective and disciplined 12th man than me. He also used to love going on and doing a bit of fielding, whereas surprisingly that wasn't really my forte.

On one occasion we were away at Bath against Gloucestershire and Phil Edmonds was playing towards the end of his career. Phil could be a bit of a difficult character – sounds like something my teachers might have said about me! – and had a lot going on when it came to his other business interests and things like that, and Mike Gatting was getting increasingly hacked off with it all. During this game Phil kept ducking off the field to go and make phone calls, and Gussy kept having to replace him as the fielder. About the third time he did it, Gatt turned to Gus and said: 'What the bloody hell are you doing back on here?!'

'Edmonds has gone off again so I'm fielding for him,' said our beanpole 12th man.

'Right, the next time he calls you on, you stay put, understand?'

'How can I tell him I'm not replacing him when he's an England bowler, a stalwart of the club and I'm just a young lad starting my career,' was Gussy's reply.

'I don't care. The next time he tells you to come on, you tell him to f**k off. You don't come on for him anymore,' said Gatt.

At which point Phil came back on the field and an almighty row erupted between him and the skipper, which actually held up play for a few minutes. Things settled down and then at lunch Gatt made it quite clear that he wasn't to come off to make his business calls anymore, and that was that. He signed off the conversation by telling Edmonds: 'And you can f**k off down to third man while you're at it.'

We went back on after lunch and in the first over the batsman poked one down to third man where Edmonds was fielding, while Gatt was fielding at gully. It was a nice easy single, but for some reason Edmonds came tearing in, picked the ball up and,

from about 30 yards away, absolutely hurled the ball with everything he could straight at Gatt's head.

It went like a bullet and Gatt had no choice but to hit the deck
to get out of the way and was left spread-eagled across the outfield.
After which Gatt got up and we all expected him to explode
again. Instead, he just looked at Edmonds, gave him the wanker
sign and got on with the game as if nothing had happened.

Their run-ins were a bit of a feature of the Middlesex dressing
room in those days and Phil did take the piss a bit. He used to
schedule his meetings during the lunch and tea breaks and go
off for half an hour to sort out a bit of business before coming
back and playing. It was quite ridiculous really, and when he
announced that he only wanted to play at Lord's, so that he
could stay in London and work on other things, then it was
time to call it a day.

What reminds me of that escapade between Edmonds and
Gatting down at Bath was a little disagreement I had with
Duncan Fletcher during my career, although I believe I was well
within my rights. He had this exercise he used to do after training. He'd pick one of the lads and you had to take 10 catches
before being allowed to go back into the pavilion. Now, I don't
mind trying to take 10 catches if in fact you give me the chance
to actually catch the ball. What Fletcher did was hit the ball just
out of reach, so you would either run forward or run backwards
to try and catch it. Ultimately, though, it would be just beyond
reach, and the closer you got to the ball without catching it then
the happier Fletcher would be. It was the FCW test, where the
first two letters stood for well-known swear words with -ing
attached to them, and the last was another well-worn term
ending in -ker!

As you can imagine, this was hardly my cup of tea, yet on the tour to South Africa in 1999 it was unavoidable. It was also a chance for those lucky enough not to be picked to sit and watch the show, guffawing and taking the piss throughout. 'C'mon, Tufnell, let's see you catch ten,' Fletcher said with a bit too much of a smile for my liking.

Up went the first one and I didn't even get a hand to it. Then the next and the third went the same way, as he had me running this way and that. Eventually I caught one and the ironic cheers weren't wasted on me.

It would take five more attempts before I got my second, and already I was beginning to get fed up with it. I mean, if you want me to do some sprints and some running about then fine, but don't dress it up in an exercise that is designed to humiliate people. The next catch went up and again it was just short. In my anger, I hurled the ball much like Phil Edmonds did at Gatt all those years before, but my aim wasn't great and it flew just out of Fletcher's reach.

Even though there was brilliant sunshine, I could still see the light bulb that went off in my head as Fletcher missed that ball. He only had three at his feet and I worked out that if they all went over his head, he wouldn't have anything left to torment me with. One by one I threw them high over his head, each time with a 'Sorry, Fletch', just like he gave me. As the last one went, I said, 'Sorry, Fletch. Oh, it looks like you've run out of balls. I guess that will be that.'

'Don't you go anywhere, Tufnell. I'll get the balls and you wait there.'

That was it, this was now a battle of wills, him slapping the balls out of my reach and me throwing them out of his. It was pretty pathetic really, but I was being made to look like a complete mug. Eventually I said, 'Sod this, I've had enough,' and walked off.

'Just as I thought, Tufnell,' came the smug reply.

It was the low point of my relationship with Duncan. That Test match was hailed as a triumph for sportsmanship before ultimately being revealed as a fix by Hansie Cronje, but for me it will always be the FCW Test.

When it comes to finger spinners, only the very, very best survive. You can't turn it as much as a wrist spinner, you can't disguise your variations like a mystery spinner and you can't scare the batsman like a fast bowler. You really just have a bit of turn, a bit of flight and drift, plus a whole heap of cunning to succeed. It is something that Graeme Swann is exceptional at, but before him Shaun Udal was by far the pre-eminent off spinner in the country. How he only played four Test matches in 2005 and 2006 when he made his one-day debut in 1994 is beyond me, particularly when you consider how well he performed for Hampshire throughout his career and then for Middlesex afterwards. A smart bowler with a real feel for the game and how it should be played, he produced the goods time and again on the south coast and was always a welcoming host in that part of the world, which goes a long way in my book.

SHAUN UDAL – OVERSEAS MAGIC

As much as I love English cricket and the England team, some of the very best moments I can remember as a professional cricketer for over 20 years have been provided by overseas players. And in my time I was extremely privileged to have played with two of the very best we've ever seen on our shores – Malcolm Marshall and Shane Warne. Not only were they cricketers of a rare breed, but they were fantastic men to play alongside and they taught me a lot about the game.

Back in 1990, as a young player just making my way in the game, it was a bit of a thrill to be sharing a dressing room with the great Malcolm Marshall, who was the most phenomenal fast bowler I ever saw up close. But before a day's play in Pontypridd against Glamorgan he did something that left me completely perplexed.

It must have been about five minutes before the start of play on day three. As the bell sounds and the umpires trot out, Macco is on his brick of a mobile phone, calling Stoneham Golf Club in Southampton to book a tee-off time for four o'clock that day. The game situation was that Glamorgan were about 10 runs ahead but only three wickets down, so had plenty of power to add to their score. We had not only to take the seven remaining wickets, but also to chase down whatever target they set us.

I was changing next to Tim Tremlett and I said to him, 'Why is Macco doing that? I don't understand how he thinks he can possibly get there in time. What does it mean?'

Trooper turned to me and replied, 'It means we are in for a very good morning, Shaun.'

Mark Nicholas was our captain and he said, 'Right, Malcolm, you bowl from the top end and Shaun you bowl from the other.'

That morning he bowled like I'd never seen a bowler bowl before – with pace, accuracy and more movement than most spinners get on a raging turner. It truly was a thing of beauty and it is why so many, including me, regard him as the greatest of them all. He took six for 12 in about 10 overs, or something daft like that, and I took the other wicket at the other end. It was Steve Watkin, who was cleaned up trying to smash the ball over mid-wicket, most likely because he didn't fancy getting down to face Macco at 90 miles an hour – and who would blame him.

Glamorgan only managed to get 172 by the time it was all over, which left us with 70 needed to win. Our top four of Paul Terry, Chris and Robin Smith and David Gower was more than useful, so there was no doubt in our dressing room that they would knock them off – the question was, how quickly?

Macco knew what was required and very calmly told the batsmen that they should get on with it because there was still plenty of movement and they shouldn't give the Glamorgan bowlers a chance to get among them. Also that if they didn't want him to crank it up in the nets next time they should get on with things. They didn't need much more of an incentive than that.

Just after lunch the game was won. Macco departed at 2 p.m. and at three minutes to four, having just destroyed a batting line-up that morning, he walked on to the tee at Stoneham and played 18 holes – something no mere mortal would have even contemplated much less succeeded in doing, but that was the class of the man.

There was perhaps one other man I played with who was capable of such feats, and that was Shane Warne. Warney is a guy I have nothing but admiration for, both as a player and a bloke, and I was lucky enough to play with him at the other end of my career. After everything he did for Hampshire during his time at the club, I'm only sorry we couldn't quite get over the line and win the championship while he was around.

He was so committed to the cause that, after single-handedly keeping Australia in the hunt for the Ashes in 2005 with an unbelievable 40 wickets, he then returned to Hampshire and put his shoulder through agony just to try and get us over the line. In 2005 we missed out on the title to Nottinghamshire by just 2.5 points, which is enough to make anyone cry. But not Warney – he was always smiling.

It is that smile I will never forget when he called me over to one side in Cardiff and told me to get prepared for a call-up to the England squad for that winter's tour to Pakistan. At the age of 35, the dream I had harboured for a lifetime was about to come true and Warney handled it perfectly, by making sure I wasn't overwhelmed or surprised when I got the call.

The morning the squad was due to be announced, I was waiting by the phone. Nine o'clock came and went. Then 9.30, then 9.45am and so on. To the point where I thought Warney had been winding me up. At 10.30 the phone rang and it was the chairman of selectors, David Graveney. He told me I was in and I had tears in my eyes. I told my wife and then the first call I made was to my dad, who had supported me throughout my career. I said to him, 'Dad, I'm in!'

'In what?' Talk about dampening the mood.

'I'm in the England squad, Dad!'

'What England squad?' By now I wasn't sure I'd got through to the right bloke.

'I'm going to Pakistan, Dad, on the England Test tour, to play cricket, for my country.'

'Oh, right. Well done, son, well done.' Finally.

I went round to see my mum at work, certain that I would get a better reaction. 'What's happened? Who's died?' Not quite the response, but once I told her the news, the champagne corks were popped and the celebration began. And who should call but Warney.

'Enjoy it, Shaggy, you'll be great and you'll take loads of

wickets out there. This is what you deserve, so make the most of it. Although you'll do well to find a decent golf course!'

With the Pakistan tour behind me – and despite losing that series 2–0 – I was selected to go to India on the following trip, and I really felt like it was my last chance to make an impact. Unfortunately, I wasn't picked in either of the first two matches. Ian Blackwell played as the second spinner behind Monty Panesar in the opener, and then in Mohali we played just Monty. But at one–nil down and heading to Mumbai I was given another chance to show what I could do. The first couple of days didn't really go my way and, if I'm honest, I was feeling pretty low about the whole experience.

Somehow Warney must have known this because out of the blue he called me in my hotel room and gave me the perfect pick-me-up. It was just the call I needed and was the boost of confidence that allowed me to finally show what I was capable of. The rest of the game flew by, as the dressing room pulled together to the strains of Johnny Cash's 'The Ring of Fire', our signature tune. I managed to take four for 14 as we won a rare Test in India to draw the series. It was the ultimate highlight of my career and once again I had Shane Warne to thank for his part. Aussies aren't all bad, really.

Having been captain of England myself with less than distinguished results, I have a tremendous amount of respect for those who are able to achieve success in the job by bringing the best out of themselves and those around them. Mike Brearley was able to do it time and again during my playing days, and in recent times Michael Vaughan was his equal as a captain. His crowning glory will always be the 2005 Ashes series, but he led England to much more success than that and it shouldn't be forgotten. Nor should it overshadow his brilliance as a batsman. He made it to the top of the world in that department and, before he even took over the reins, his performances with the bat in the 2002/03 Ashes series Down Under simply did not deserve to be on the losing side. Since quitting the game as a player, he's proved to be an astute pundit, a joy to play golf with, a good man to work with on charities and, even though it's not my cup of tea, he's shown he's still got a little bit of magic in those dancing feet.

MICHAEL VAUGHAN –
USE YOUR LOAF

Playing cricket, whether it is for Sheffield Collegiate, Yorkshire or England, is about shared experiences and satisfaction with your team-mates. Of course, you want to perform to the best of your ability and come away with a hundred, or five wickets, but you want those performances to go towards a team victory, because that is what validates it all.

There is no better feeling than team success and that is what we all play for. Whenever people ask me for my favourite memories of my career, it's always the knocks that went towards wins, precisely because it is after a big win that you experience those unique moments that only team sport can provide. It might be an entire night spent in a dressing room, or the celebrations that take you to the prime minister's garden – either way, they are all special. Sometimes there can be no rhyme or reason to what you get up to, and my particular favourite memory of dressing-room antics inevitably comes from that series in 2005 when we finally won the Ashes after nearly two decades without them. Surprisingly, though, the night I remember most was not following the draw at The Oval and the open-top bus ride that followed. It was actually earlier in the piece when things were just starting to get interesting.

We had lost the first Test at Lord's even though we had come out fighting. Glenn McGrath was again unplayable, and Australia deservedly won the game. There was a sense of 'here we go again' in some quarters, but I knew we were better than that and thought we stood a good chance of levelling things up. In the aftermath of Lord's, the Australian players stayed celebrating late into the day in their dressing room, and then took their families out into the middle to soak up the win. We had slipped off home pretty quickly and thought long and hard about how to hit back.

At Edgbaston Ricky Ponting made the mistake of putting us into bat, and we got off to a flyer thanks to Marcus Trescothick and Andrew Strauss. As the game evolved, we were in complete control and, by the Sunday morning, it was just a matter of time before we took the final few wickets to win. As it turned out, things got a little tighter than we would have liked. The tension was almost unbearable because we very nearly threw away a win, but thankfully we got over the line and the relief was huge. With the afternoon stretching out before us, we had a few drinks in our dressing room to celebrate, and then we took a load of beers into the Aussie room to share with them. That was a really important step for us. Not only had we beaten this great team, but we were having a drink with them as well, and it made them seem, well, human. That might sound strange but when you've been beaten from pillar to post by these guys year after year, they take on an almost mythical status, and you begin to wonder whether they are normal like you or some kind of super-cricketing gods.

After a few drinks with them, we went back to the team hotel to freshen up and then head out for a proper night's celebration. As we were on our way out of the door someone noticed a loaf of bread on the floor that had clearly fallen off a tray or out of someone's bag. Either way, it was just lying there and it was too tempting to be left alone. As I walked out of the door, Tres put boot to bread and the loaf flew out the door with me. Vaughan to Giles, Giles to Trescothick, Trescothick to Jones and back to Vaughan. We were off and running down the road, and the loaf was being passed back and forth like a ball in the 1970 World Cup and we were Brazil.

We ducked into the first bar and the loaf came with us. A couple of drinks and we were off again, and so too was the loaf. Again, the silky skills on show would have put Barcelona to shame, or at least that's what we thought in our own hazy minds. We must have popped into five or six different bars on Broad Street and on each occasion the loaf was booted in with us.

It must have been about three in the morning when I had finally had enough. It had been a cracking night, full of the joys of Test victory, and as I was about to leave the last venue, the Living Room, I had completely forgotten about the loaf. I climbed into the lift to get back to the ground floor and, on exiting, something in the corner caught my eye. It was a bruised and battered multi-seed batch. Never before had I been so happy to see a loaf of bread in my life – it had survived the night, as had I. We left the lift together; me, unsteady on my feet, yet dribbling the bread as if I were Gazza against Scotland in Euro 1996. I must have looked like a complete prat, a dishevelled crazy man talking to a loaf of bread, but I didn't care. I guided the ball/breaded goodness through the German defence/revolving door of the hotel and into the lobby, faced up to the giant goalkeeper/security guard and slotted it home into the corner of the goal/lobby as the crowd roared in delight and chanted my name/told me to go to bed.

I initially felt on top of the world thanks to the Ashes win at Edgbaston, and I stayed there thanks to a Hovis loaf. It was a good time.

Smooth as silk. That is the only way to describe our presenter Ian Ward, who has transferred from being a fine cricketer to a brilliant broadcaster with ease. If you thought Mark Nicholas made a good fist of it, or David Gower, then Wardy has set the bar. He was a useful opening batsman as a player and rightly earned a handful of Test caps in 2001. However, he ran straight into the Aussies in their pomp and didn't quite last beyond that. He wasn't the first man that happened to. Without a lengthy England career, he was able to focus on his counties, and it is no coincidence that Surrey won County Championship titles with him there and Sussex won titles when he moved to the south coast. He is a team man of the highest quality and we get to see that day in, day out at Sky Sports, where he has become an invaluable part of the crew.

IAN WARD – GOOD-LOOKING FINES

Dressing rooms are unusual places. They are full of men who play the sport they have loved since they were kids, and as such a big part of it remains childish. Even though we are professional, and work bloody hard to get to where we are, the dressing room itself can be a fun place full of laughter and silly behaviour that just wouldn't seem normal in most other work-places. Perhaps it is to help relieve the stress of the job out on the field, or maybe it is just because groups of men behave like boys – either way, you get plenty of ups and downs and the team becomes your family.

When I played for Surrey, I was lucky enough to play in one of the greatest sides the county has produced. There was plenty of home-grown talent on show too – men like Alec Stewart, Graham Thorpe, Alex Tudor and Martin Bicknell. We won everything going and it was a great time for the club. But it hadn't always been that way, and we actually had to put our house in order before we started winning trophies.

It took an Aussie coach by the name of Dave Gilbert to bring it all together, with the help of Adam Hollioake as our skipper. In my early days we had a few issues with discipline, not outrageous ones, just with stuff like timekeeping and dress code, which make a difference in terms of the attitude you have. Dave, or Lizard as we called him, was adamant that things would need to change if we were going to be successful, insisting that with the amount of talent we had in our dressing room we had no excuse for failing to win something every year.

So we all agreed to a new fines system, which would penalise people quite harshly for even minor offences. You could end up losing quite a bit if you were even five minutes late for a meeting or training session. We also put in place a new dress code to make sure people turned up wearing the right kit at the right time. It was going to take a bit of getting used to, but everyone bought into it, and it made a noticeable difference. Obviously, there were going to be some who fitted into it more easily than others. Stewie had no problem; not only does he hate giving money away, he is also the most organised and well-turned-out cricketer in the history of the game. Someone like Adam's brother, Ben, found it a little bit trickier.

Ben Hollioake was a terrific cricketer, with bundles of talent with both bat and ball, the sort of cricketer everyone wants to

258

have in their team. But with his laid-back character, things like timekeeping were an inconvenience. Midway through the season, Ben had already lost plenty of money for being late and/or wearing the wrong kit, and it was eating into his funds for going out and that was the real punishment for him. He was determined to get it right. However, one weekend we had a Sunday League match and Ben was running late. Aware of the time, he simply grabbed whatever kit he could lay his hands on and ran out of the door. Better to be on time in the wrong clothes, he thought.

At The Oval there are two entrances to the dressing room: one through the front that looks out over the pitch, the other round the back through the dining room that sits behind it. As Ben sprinted up the stairs to get to the dressing room on time, he realised he would just make it, but he was now regretting not turning up in the right kit so he didn't go in through the front. He went into the dining room, where the dinner ladies were getting lunch ready, dropped his bag and then dropped his trousers. Off came the t-shirt, the boxers and the socks – the younger Hollioake was standing in what he came into the world wearing: absolutely nothing. The ladies got a good eyeful, and I can tell you they were talking about it for weeks afterwards. Ben was a good-looking lad and both he and they knew it.

In the dressing room, Lizard was telling us how he had already seen Ben and knew he wasn't wearing the right kit, so if anyone had lent him theirs they would get fined, too. Just then the door opened and Ben strolled in, with hands on hips and a giant grin on his face. 'You can't fine me, boss, I'm on time and I'm not wearing the wrong kit. I'm not wearing any kit!' he declared.

Beefy's Cricket Tales

Everyone was in fits of laughter and, to Lizard's credit, instead of a reprimand, Ben got off scot-free. He managed to keep a bit of cash in his pocket – even though he didn't have any.

That was Ben all over, a guy you couldn't stay mad at. He always had an easy charm and a way of getting you on his side. His sad passing before his time hit everyone who shared that dressing room with him hard, but at least we have some great memories like this.

Shane Warne is the greatest spinner ever to have played the game and he single-handedly rejuvenated the art of spin bowling around the world. He is also a great bloke.

Warney has become a good mate of mine since we first did a Nike commercial together back in the 1990s. His outlook on the game and on life is very similar to mine. We're here to have a good time, compete as hard as possible on the pitch and enjoy ourselves off it, and he has certainly done that. He also genuinely cares about the game and the people who play it. He understands that it is the players who the public come to see and for that reason they must be entertained. Few Australians have given the world as much entertainment as him.

SHANE WARNE – SOMETHING SMELLS GOOD

During my time in the Aussie team, I had the pleasure to play with some sensational cricketers and some unbelievable blokes. For the vast majority of my time in the Australian dressing room I was laughing or smiling, because it was always full of life, full of banter, and with one or two characters like Merv Hughes thrown in, you couldn't help but enjoy yourself.

There were moments with Merv when he would have me in such stitches that I didn't think I'd be able to bowl; and at other times he would play jokes on me that I swore never to forgive him for. But, of course, five minutes later it was all fine. On one occasion, we were sharing a room together and we both fancied a burger and chips from room service, so that's what we ordered. After we'd finished, we had to put the tray outside the room for the hotel staff to pick up. The only problem was that in those days our fitness coach, Errol Alcock, used to prowl around the corridors checking to see what the players had been eating, so we didn't want any evidence of our burger and chips to be outside our door.

Merv said: 'Warney, why don't you just pop the tray outside, but leave it a couple of doors down so Errol doesn't know it was ours.'

'Good idea, Merv,' I said.

It just so happened I was ready for bed by now, and I like to sleep in my birthday suit, so I was completely naked as I got up to take the tray out. I could have chucked on a pair of shorts or something to do the job, but the truth is I was just lazy and couldn't be bothered. In any case, I was only going out of the room for all of 10 seconds.

As I placed the tray on the floor two doors down, I heard a click. Merv had leapt up and shut the door behind me. I couldn't believe he had done that to me. I was knocking on the door ferociously, whispering, 'Merv, Merv, let me in.'

'Sorry, what? I can't hear you,' came the reply.

'Aw, come on, Merv, let me in – it's not funny. Someone could be here any minute.'

I couldn't really shout too loudly because other people in their rooms would have come out. He left me out there for fully five minutes, although it felt like 50, and only when I told him Allan Border was coming did he let me back in.

There have been a few practical jokers in the Aussie dressing rooms over the years, but there was one joke that took aim at John Buchanan but backfired on all of us, and to this day no one knows who was responsible. Buck was our coach during one of our most successful periods, and it's fair to say he had some unique views on the game and the way to play it. A few of the guys in the team thought he made a lot of sense, but there were also a few of us who felt he made things a little more complicated than was necessary. Regardless of whether or not you saw eye to eye with him, the fact remains he was involved when we produced some of our best cricket and that will never change.

One year, we were playing in Perth and the next match was due to be in Adelaide – which meant that as soon as the game was over, we'd pack up our kit and it would be driven across the Nullarbor Plain to Adelaide. It takes 24 hours to drive across there and the backroom guys would slog it out in the van in temperatures that hit 50 degrees. It is a harsh environment.

Anyway, in the dressing room in Perth we used to have some fabulous fresh seafood laid out for us on platters. Some gorgeous prawns and fresh fish to nibble at during the lunch and tea breaks. Well, some bright spark thought it would be a good idea to lob a few prawns into John Buchanan's cricket bag before it got packed up with 20 others and carted off to Adelaide in the van.

We then flew in a few days later and all these bags were sitting in the dressing room, waiting to be opened. Well, you can imagine the stench that filled the room as Buck opened his bag and released the aroma into the air. For the next five or six days during the Test match the dressing room stank like rancid fish, so all the boys spent the entire game either in the field or watching from the balcony. One of the commentators said it showed unbelievable togetherness and spirit in the Aussie team, because we were all out there watching the game. If only he knew.

Robert George Dylan Willis was one of the greatest fast bowlers England has ever produced and he is one of the best friends I have ever made. His figures stand up against any other bowler, but what they don't tell you is how tough Bob was and how much he went through to take those wickets. Fast bowling is an awkward occupation at the best of times, but try doing it when you're as gangly and as awkward as Bob was! Yet when he got it right he was poetry in motion, and thankfully for England he got it right more often than not. We shared some amazing times on the field and some equally enjoyable ones off it, none more so than the night before that Headingley turnaround in 1981, when we were dancing in each other's arms thinking it would be our last match together. Instead, it became our best match together and we've stayed close ever since.

BOB WILLIS – BOTHAM THE MANCHILD

Ian Botham is a pain. Or, more accurately, playing cricket with Ian Botham was painful. It didn't matter where you were, whether you were playing or not, Ian had a way of making an impact. I think it stems from his low boredom threshold, coupled with his insatiable and total belief in himself, which makes for a dangerous combination. Where the rest of us grew up and realised our limitations, Ian has never accepted them, and that is why he was the player he was. A moment's self-doubt and it could have all been so very different.

We have been good friends for a while now, but it didn't start out that way – due, shall we say, to his overexuberance. There are a few old dressing-room tricks that players play on each other and more often than not it involves cutting some item or other – but that was too mundane for Ian. He was a boisterous figure from the moment he walked into the dressing room, but he really burst into life on his first tour to New Zealand in 1978, when he collected wickets galore as well as his first Test ton.

Fresh from that hundred he took five wickets as we dominated the Kiwis, but we narrowly failed to enforce the follow on. We had a healthy lead of 183 and knew we wouldn't need too many more to bowl them out a second time on a wearing pitch.

Mike Brearley had gone home and left Geoff Boycott in charge. We'd made a balls-up of the first Test and so needed to strike back quickly and positively, but in those days Geoffrey didn't do anything quickly or positively, which meant trouble. Instead of pushing on with the run rate, Boycs was taking his time, and the rest of the senior players were getting restless. The only solution to try and get things moving was for someone to run him out if another wicket fell, but who would do it?

Step forward Ian, who didn't need asking twice. I think he was quite glad of the chance to show off in front of the rest of the team and, boy, did he do so in spectacular style. Poor old Boycs fell for Ian's 'to-me, to-you' Chuckle Brother routine and came trudging back in with a face like thunder. He sat in silence in the dressing room, with a towel over his head. Ian was busy giving it a bit of a thrash and getting us a big enough lead to try and bowl them out and win the game. The only problem was that Boycs was refusing to talk to anyone, so he wouldn't even go and tell the Kiwis that we were declaring. When he eventually came round, he was adamant that the declaration was another set-up. He was worried about losing the game so much that we had to really badger him to declare. Thankfully, he did and we went on to win the game by 174 runs.

It was an extra-eventful game because it was where Ian played his first prank on me, and it was not to be the last.

Whenever we batted, I used to like to relax and settle down with a cup of tea and a newspaper before even having to think about batting. New Zealand is the perfect spot for that, especially as they had the knack of finding lovely comfortable chairs and sofas for the bowlers to melt into and put their feet up. We had just bowled New Zealand out for 235 and Ian had taken five wickets to go with his hundred, so he was excitable to say the least. But he was still a junior member of the dressing room, so you'd have thought he'd behave with a bit of decorum. No chance.

I had just taken my kit off after bowling and settled down in a pair of shorts to read my paper. Ian came up to me and offered to make me a cup of tea. I accepted, and all was well in my world. A few moments later Ian sidled up to me and offered me my mug of tea; as he gave it to me he withdrew the metal spoon from the boiling liquid and placed the utensil directly on to my bare leg. You can imagine the reaction: I yelped, jumped up and threw most of the mug of tea all over myself, thus getting a double helping of heat-related pain. It couldn't have worked better from Ian's point of view, as he ran off laughing. I was less than impressed.

I soon discovered that he didn't really care about the consequences, as long as he got his target. It meant you just had to have your wits about you when he was around. And, of course, you usually made your own tea. After a spell of trying and failing to get me with the teaspoon, he graduated to something altogether more spectacular. While reading a newspaper on that same trip, I was enjoying a particularly good feature on music when suddenly my fingers became hot. Ian had set fire to the paper and it literally disintegrated in my hands. Unlike the teaspoon, everyone could see what he had done, and the fact that they were all rolling about laughing gave Ian the validation to do it again. And he did. Again and again and again.

It was like sharing a dressing room with a big kid. I tried shouting at him, it didn't work; I tried ignoring him, it didn't work; so I tried reasoning with him and that didn't work, either. You just had to find a way to put up with him and hope he targeted someone else. The thing is, while he was having fun off the field, he was winning us matches on it, so you couldn't really complain about what he got up to, and that was the way I looked at it. He was our match-winner and our dressing-room joker, and the two went hand in hand.

It has continued to this day in the Sky Sports commentary box, where he now terrorises players who didn't manage to play with him but who've heard the stories and are on their guard, especially if Ian has been on the receiving end of a bit of banter himself. I must admit I enjoyed visiting the box a couple of years ago, just around the time that Saddam Hussein had been found in a hole and captured in Tikrit – a town in Iraq. Ian was adamant that he'd been caught off the coast of Greece in Crete! At that point I should have put him right, but instead, just before I left, I nodded and said how terrible it was that the Greeks had hidden him like that. He was off and running, telling all and sundry just what he thought of the Greek islands as a result, and no one could quite understand what he was talking about.

He took a bit of a hammering that day from the boys in the box over his geography. When I met him for dinner that night, he asked me why on earth I hadn't corrected him and told about the right place. I said, 'If you'd bothered to read newspapers rather than burn them, you might have an idea of the difference between the two!'

Behind every great sportsman is a great sportswriter and I've been lucky enough to have a fair few over the years. Whether it was my partner in crime, Chris Lander, who joined me on the first ever charity walk, or 'Machine Gun' Mike Walters (for his rat-a-tat speech), I've had a blast with them all. And there is no change with my current 'ghost', Dean Wilson, who has kept my words in tiptop shape. As a bona fide member of the press pack, he's heard plenty of dressing-room stories down the years, and by jogging my memory he's helped bring many of them to life within these pages. There might be a frustrated cricketer in there somewhere, striving to get out, but the journalist in him is flourishing just fine.

DEAN WILSON – CARS

For any budding young cricketer the dream is to make it as a professional and then ultimately play for England. Failing that, the next best thing is to write about it and follow the England team around the world.

In my case, as with so many others, being a useful schoolboy cricketer with a penchant for striking fours and sixes wasn't quite enough to sustain a playing career, so after university a proper job beckoned. Thankfully, that proper job has turned out to be the chance to travel up and down the UK, and around the world, following the fortunes of the England cricket team. It is not quite as glamorous as people think, but yes, I know, I'm a lucky boy to be doing it.

Ian Botham

As you might hope and expect, there was a bit of studying to be done to get here, working my way through school and university. But along the way there was plenty of cricket played as well, and watching former team-mates and opponents go on to make it as professionals has been great to see. During my first year at Birmingham University, current Warwickshire captain, Jim Troughton, was an undergraduate and played in the team that made it as far as the semi-finals of the British Universities tournament. His left-arm spin had worked a treat for us in restricting Cambridge University in the quarter-final at Fenner's, but the rain got in the way and we had to replay the game.

Another washout meant that the only option was to have a bowl-out on the morning of the semi-final, with the winner staying on at The Parks to play the University of the West of England, and the loser going home. It was a pretty high standard of bowling, with five bowlers given two chances each per team. After the very best that the two sides had to offer had each sent down their pair of deliveries, Birmingham had triumphed by the Barry Davies scoreline of 1–0.

We went on to play the semi-final immediately and happened to be fielding first. On our return to the dressing room at the end of the innings we discovered that something was amiss. Bags had been opened and at first there was a real fear that valuables had been taken. As it happened, nothing had been stolen, but all our towels were hanging up on the pegs. Not only that, but they were also wet and dirty. A parting gift from the Cambridge side, who clearly didn't take too kindly to being beaten by their redbrick opponents ... A Cambridge team that contained current England assistant coach, Richard Halsall.

It was a pretty harmless prank, to be honest, and everyone reacted well. But by far and away the best reaction I've ever seen to misfortune was Dougie Brown's. The Warwickshire and England all-rounder was invited to be guest speaker at our university cricket club dinner. He was brilliant. Interacting well with all the students beforehand, delivering a great speech and then taking a few questions afterwards. The players had lined up a party to crack on to – your typical student club night at the guild, laced with pints of snakebite. So, as the function drew to a close, imagine my surprise when Dougie not only asked where we were headed, but whether he was invited, too. Of course he was!

Ready to jump into a cab, he just had to pop something into the car he'd parked at the function room, only to discover that someone had tried to break into it. There was a crack in the back windscreen, scratches along the door panel, and the lock had been fiddled with and was dented. The car looked a bit of a mess. The police were called and statements were taken. Clearly upset by the incident, Dougie sorted things out with the security guard at the venue, and asked for a cab to be called, presumably to take him home. Not a chance of it. Ten minutes later, he was on the dance floor, drink in hand, as if nothing had happened. If ever someone could put a golden duck out of their minds, it had to be him.

Sportsmen and their cars are just one of those relationships that seem to be doomed from the start. The heady combination of youth, money and adrenaline is a potent, often dangerous, mix, but that is all part of growing up. For the more serene members of the press corps, driving is more of a function than a status symbol, and it is often the best way to get about when on tour. A particular favourite is New Zealand, where you can drive to any venue very easily, even taking the Picton ferry if you want to get between the islands.

Back in 2008 this was the transport of choice for most of us and we split up, two to a car, as we made our way around one of the world's most beautiful countries. My co-driver for the tour was Angus Fraser, the former England bowler, who could occasionally be a little grumpy with the world but who was an interesting and chatty enough travel companion.

He also played a couple of winters for a club in Wellington, so he knew the country very well indeed. Everything had worked pretty well throughout the trip, picking up and dropping off the cars as and when, until we collected our car for the last, long journey from Wellington to Napier for the final Test match.

Gus was unhappy because the car hire company had given us a compact Ford Focus when he'd specifically requested something bigger. This was because his family were flying out to join him for the end of the tour, after which they would be going on a bit of a driving holiday for a couple of weeks and he was keeping the car for that. There was nothing available at Wellington, so arrangements were made for an alternative car to be ready for us in a day or two in Napier – no problem.

We set off out of town, looking to pick up State Highway 2, which would take us all the way. It is not a particularly taxing drive, with large sections being just a very straight road. The speed limit is 100 kmph. Despite driving a fairly small-engine car, Gus was determined to get the pedal to the metal and, with the strains of T-Rex on the stereo, he managed to get us well over that mark on the speedometer.

As for what happened next, you can probably guess. We were clocked by a police car going the other way and were asked to pull over. This was the conversation that ensued.

Officer: 'Excuse me, sir, do you know how fast you were driving?'

Fraser: 'Oh, not sure, about ninety-five?'

Officer: 'No, sir, you were not. It was a hundred and forty-four.'

Fraser: 'Don't be so ridiculous, this car's not capable of going that fast.'

Officer: 'I'm afraid it is, sir, and since you were doing more than forty over the limit I'm going to have to ask you for your licence.'

Fraser: 'This is bloody stupid, I was never going that fast. You need to check your equipment. Haven't you got anything better to do.'

Officer: 'The licence please, sir.'

Fraser: 'For f**k's sake, can't we come to some arrangement?'

Officer: 'I don't know what you're suggesting or accusing me of, sir, but please hand over your licence and step out of the car.'

Fifteen minutes later, the officer had taken Gus's licence, given him a breathalyser test (he hadn't been drinking) and written out a ticket that forbade him from driving in New Zealand and required him to apply for the return of his licence once he was back home.

To call him grumpy for the rest of the journey would be an understatement.

Fraser: 'Come on, grandad, put your foot down, will you? I'd like to get to Napier before dark.'

Me: 'I think we've lost enough driving licences for one day, don't you? By the way, I guess your wife is going to be really happy to drive around the wine region of New Zealand for the next two weeks . . .'

Fraser: 'Oh f**k!'